## "A SPECTRE IS HAUNTING EUROPE—THE SPECTRE OF COMMUNISM . . ."

With these words, in 1848, Karl Marx began the *Manifesto* that would in time make Communism a force shadowing the entire globe.

Many of the *Manifesto*'s predictions of war and disorder have proven to be tragically correct. Many of its prescriptions for change have been attempted with results that have been as major in scope as they have been debatable in value.

Today its eloquence remains undiminished—and its powers of persuasion potent. We owe it to ourselves to understand what it really says and where its appeal lies, if we are to understand and deal with the world it has so profoundly influenced.

## *Harold J. Laski on* THE COMMUNIST MANIFESTO

**HAROLD J. LASKI** was one of the most distinguished scholars and influential political thinkers of our time, in addition to playing an active role in the British Labor Party.

**T. B. BOTTOMORE** is head of the Department of Political Science, Sociology, and Anthropology at Simon Fraser University, Canada; and author of *Classes in Modern Society* and (with Maximilien Rubel) *Karl Marx: Selected Writings in Sociology and Social Philosophy.*

## SIGNET CLASSIC and MENTOR Titles of Interest

# Harold J. Laski
## on
# THE COMMUNIST MANIFESTO

*An Introduction*

*Together with the Original Text
and Prefaces by*

**Karl Marx
and
Friedrich Engels**

**Foreword for the American Edition
by T. B. Bottomore**

A MENTOR BOOK
**NEW AMERICAN LIBRARY**
TIMES MIRROR
New York

© Copyright, 1967, by Random House, Inc.

All rights reserved. For information address Pantheon Books, Inc.,
a division of Random House, Inc., 201 East 50th Street,
New York, New York 10022.

This is an authorized reprint of a hardcover edition published by
Pantheon Books, Inc. A hardcover edition was published in
England by George Allen & Unwin, Ltd.

Library of Congress Catalog Card Number: 82-81660

 MENTOR TRADEMARK REG. U.S. PAT. OFF. AND FOREIGN COUNTRIES
REGISTERED TRADEMARK—MARCA REGISTRADA
HECHO EN CHICAGO, U.S.A.

SIGNET, SIGNET CLASSICS, MENTOR, PLUME, MERIDIAN AND NAL
BOOKS are published by The New American Library, Inc.,
1633 Broadway, New York, New York 10019.

First Mentor Printing, June, 1982

1   2   3   4   5   6   7   8   9

PRINTED IN THE UNITED STATES OF AMERICA

# *Foreword*

THIS EDITION of the *Communist Manifesto*, issued by the British Labour Party in 1948 to mark the centenary of the original publication, is without question the best available in the English language. The text of the *Manifesto* is that of the authorised English translation of 1888, edited and annotated by Engels, and it is preceded by several prefaces—to the 1888 translation, to the German editions of 1872, 1883 and 1890, and to the Russian edition of 1882—in which Marx and Engels amplified and modified some of the ideas which they had expressed in 1848. The introduction to this volume, by the late Harold Laski, provides the most thorough historical and critical study of the *Manifesto* since Charles Andler's introduction and commentary for the French edition of 1901 and D. Riazanov's historical introduction to the French translation by J. Molitor in 1934; and it benefits, in comparison with these two works, from the greater knowledge of the sources of Marx's ideas and from the experience of the vicissitudes of Marxist social theory which became available during the first half of the twentieth century.

Laski discusses, in fact, three subjects. The first is the historical background of the *Manifesto*, which is traced both in the intellectual sphere, in the earlier writings of Marx and Engels (particularly *The German Ideology*) which reveal the gradual development of their distinctive conception of society, and in the sphere of politics, in the progress of the socialist movement among revolutionary exiles and its connections with working-class organizations.

The second subject is the content of the *Manifesto*, and especially the political doctrine and political strategy which it expounds. Laski examines Marx and Engels' theory of revolutionary class struggle, their views on the role of violence in bringing about fundamental social changes, and their conception of the "dictatorship of the proletariat." These ideas, as formulated in the *Manifesto* and subsequently qualified by Marx and Engels in the light of their experience of the Paris Commune, the advance of legal socialist parties, notably in Germany, and the gradual extension of the suffrage in the advanced capitalist countries, Laski then contrasts with the ideas introduced subsequently by Lenin, particularly in *State and Revolution*, and their practical working out in Russia after 1917.

This discussion leads on to the third main theme, which is the fate of Marxist doctrine after it had become the state-orthodoxy of a ruling party in the U.S.S.R., and when in Laski's words "the large and flexible outlook of the *Communist Manifesto* is applied in a narrow and dogmatically rigid way." There is a brief and incisive account of the intellectual petrifaction and political irresponsibility of the Communist parties in the West during the period of Stalin's rule; against which Laski properly balances the generally fructifying influence of Marxist thought in socialist movements which are as diverse as the circumstances of the countries in which they exist.

After nearly twenty years Laski's essay retains its value as a brilliant review of the rise, diffusion and practical implementation of a social doctrine which dominated the political life of mankind throughout a whole century, in a way which few, if any, other creeds have done. In these twenty years, however, social changes have taken place which necessitate a fresh consideration of some of the matters which Laski discussed in the closing pages of his essay. Today, Marxist orthodoxy lies in ruins, and it is most unlikely that it will ever be reconstituted. Marxist theory no longer arouses the same interest in its character as a rigorous guide to political action; it is more closely and critically studied as a science of society, as a canon of method, and as the vehicle through which a new social ideal has been expressed. In these aspects Marxism now affords the opportunity for dialogue between diverse schools of socialism, and between the exponents of various types of social theory, as well as renewing the long debate about the connections between thought and practice in social life.

On the other side, Laski's view of the prospects of socialism and capitalism may now seem to have been too strongly influenced by the immediate post-war circumstances and especially the advent of a Labour Government in Britain. "All over the world," he writes, "the crises of capitalism have grown both more frequent and more profound . . . the central problem is the sheer misery of the masses; and our experience makes it clear that, within a capitalist framework, there is little likelihood of its effective mitigation." We live now in a period of managed capitalism, of welfare, of the—more or less—mixed economy; and the advanced industrial countries have succeeded, since the war, in avoiding major economic crises. The great social problems which we confront seem to fall into two categories: those of the affluent industrial societies, which are seeking a way of life beyond the simple accumulation of material wealth, and those of the developing countries, which are trying to raise living standards, establish democracy, and avoid some of the evils of earlier processes of industrialization. To all these problems socialist and Marxist thought is still relevant—in the industrial countries, as the source of a new idea of social relationships, based upon equality, and in the developing countries as a guide to the planning of economic growth—but it will be, if it persists, a body of thought very different from that which was so profoundly coloured by the experience of the 1930's and which found one of its last formulations in Laski's work.

T. B. BOTTOMORE

# Contents

# *Preface*

In the spring of this year the National Executive Committee of the Labour Party decided to celebrate the centenary of the *Communist Manifesto* by the publication of a new edition with an historical introduction and illustrative material. At their request I undertook this task.

What is now published is only the *Manifesto* itself and the historical introduction. In the present circumstances it has seemed better to postpone the publication of the illustrative material, and a considerable body of notes, until the paper situation is less difficult; and I have also refrained from printing the very considerable annotated bibliography I have prepared. I hope these will appear in a separate pamphlet at a later date.

It is only necessary to add that, for English readers, by far the best lives of Marx and Engels are those by F. Mehring and Gustav Mayer respectively. They are of irreplaceable value in seeking to put the *Manifesto* in its full biographical perspective.

H.J.L.

*London, 3 November 1947*

# INTRODUCTION TO THE COMMUNIST MANIFESTO

*by Harold J. Laski*

# *Introduction*

## I

THE *Communist Manifesto* was published in February, 1848. Of its two authors, Karl Marx was then in his thirtieth, and Friedrich Engels in his twenty-eighth, year. Both had already not only a wide acquaintance with the literature of socialism, but intimate relations with most sections of the socialist agitation in Western Europe. They had been close friends for four years; each of them had published books and articles that are landmarks in the history of socialist doctrine. Marx had already had a stormy career as a journalist and social philosopher; he was already sufficiently a thorn in the side of reactionary governments to have been a refugee in both Paris and Brussels. Engels, his military service over, and his conversion to socialism completed after he had accepted the view of Moses Hess that the central problem of German philosophy was the social question, and that it could only be solved in socialist terms, had already passed nearly fifteen months of

3

his commercial training in his father's firm in Manchester by the end of 1843. He had gained a deep insight into English conditions. He had come to understand the meaning of the conflict between the major political parties, the significance of Irish nationalism, then under the leadership of Daniel O'Connell, and all the stresses and strains within the Chartist Movement; he appreciated the meaning of Chartism, and he had joined its ranks. He realised how great had been both the insight and the influence of Robert Owen. He had been an eager reader of the *Northern Star*, and had been on friendly terms, after the summer of 1843, with George Julian Harney, then, under Feargus O'Connor, the main influence on the paper, and one of the few Chartists aware of conditions and movements on the European Continent. He had written a good deal in Owen's paper, *The New Moral World*, among his contributions being a very able essay on Carlyle's *Chartism*, and a really remarkable attack on the classical political economy. In the months of his return to Barmen, from the autumn to the end of the winter of 1844–45, he had published his classic *Condition of the Working Class in England*, influenced, no doubt, by the earlier and interesting work of Buret,[1] but with a freshness and a power of philosophic generalisation far beyond Buret's grasp. He had already become certain that the antagonism between the middle classes and the proletariat was the essential clue to the history of the future.

No partnership in history is more famous than

[1] *La Misère des Classes Laboreuses en France et en Angleterre* (Paris, 1840. 2 volumes).

that of Marx and Engels, and the qualities of each were complementary to those of the other. Marx was essentially the thinker, who slowly, even with anguish, wrestled his way to the heart of a problem. At times a writer of remarkable brilliance, he was not seldom difficult and obscure because his thought went too fast or too deep for words. Erudite in an exceptional degree—his pre-eminence in scholarship was recognised by all the young Hegelians of his German years—he had something of the German gelehrte's impractical nature, a passion for systematisation, not a little of that capacity for stormy ill-temper which often comes from the nervous exhaustion of a mind which cannot cease from reflection. He had fantastic tenacity of mind, a passion for leadership, a yearning, never really satisfied, for action; born of the difficulties he encountered from the outset of his career, he had too, a brooding melancholy, a thirst for recognition, which made him too often suspicious and proud, and, despite the noble self-sacrifice of his life, in a special way a self-centered personality who, outside his family, and a very small circle of friends of whom Engels, was always the most intimate, found it, normally, much easier to give others his contempt or his hate than his respect and his affection. There were deeply lovable traits in Marx's character; but they emerge much more clearly in his private life than in his capacity either as agitator or as social philosopher. All his immense power, moreover, both of diagnosis and of strategy, rarely enabled him to conceal his inner conviction of intellectual superiority, so as to remain on easy terms with the rank and file in each phase of the movement he was eager—mostly selflessly eager—to dominate.

Engels had a quick and ready mind. He was always friendly, usually optimistic, with great gifts both for practical action and for getting on with others. He knew early where he wanted to go, but he had the self-knowledge to recognise that he could neither travel alone, nor be the leader of the expedition. Widely read, with a very real talent for moving rapidly through a great mass of material, he was facile rather than profound. He was utterly devoid of jealousy or vanity. He had a happy nature which never agonised over the difficulties of thought. After a brief moment of doubt at their first meeting, he accepted the position of *fidus Achates* to Marx, and it never occurred to him, during the friendship of forty years, marked only by one brief misunderstanding, to question his duty to serve Marx in every way he could. He was a better organiser than Marx; he had a far more immediate sense of the practical necessities of a situation. He was far quicker in seeing what to do than to recognise the deep-rooted historical relations out of which the necessity for action had developed. If Marx showed him vistas of philosophy he had never realised, he explained to Marx economic realities with a first-hand insight Marx could otherwise hardly have obtained. Not least, he made Marx see the significance of Great Britain in the historical evolution of the mid-nineteenth century at a time when Marx still thought of Germany as the central factor in its development. Without him Marx would have been in any case a great social philosopher of the Left; with him it became possible for Marx to combine superb intellectual achievement with immense practical influence. Their partnership was made when the practitioners of socialism were incoherent groups of doctrine and of agitation. When it ended they had laid the foundations of a world movement which had a well-integrated philosophy of history, and a clear method of action for the future directly born of that philosophy.

When Marx and Engels, then, came to write the *Communist Manifesto* they were not only close friends, but they combined an insight built on firm philosophic foundations with a breadth and depth of historical and contemporary knowledge unequalled in their day in its relevance to the problems of social development. They had both been enchanted by the Hegelian dialectic; they had both been driven, almost from the moment of their original acquaintance with it, first to the Hegelian Left, and then beyond it to the point where, as Marx said, it was necessary to stand Hegel on his head. They both knew from intimate personal acquaintance the deep tyranny of the German princes, always dull, always petty, and always bureaucratic. They both saw that the state-power was used to maintain a special system of legal relations which were set in a given historical mode of production; and they had both realised that nothing could be expected from the aristocracy, and little from the middle classes, except what the proletariat became self-conscious enough to realise it must take. They both understood that, without this self-consciousness, nothing could prevent the exploitation of the wage-earners by their masters; and that every social agency, from the pietism of the Churches, through the pressure of the newspapers and the censorship exercised over them, to the brutal and deliberate use of the army and the police, would be employed to break any rebellion against this exploitation. They knew that every society was a class-society, that its education, its justice, its habits, were limited by their subordination to the demands of the class which owned the instruments of economic power. They had come to see, in the famous aphorism of Marx, that "the ruling ideas of an age were the ideas of its ruling class." They had come to see also that freedom is never given from above, but must be taken from below; yet it can only be taken by men who had philosophy as well as habit. They had both seen through the hollowness of the official churches, and measured the gap between their actual and official practice. Not least, as Marx was later to add to his famous addition to the *Theses in Feuerbach*, they had had both come to have an intensely practical view of the mission of philosophy. "Hitherto," Marx was to write, "it was the mission of philosophers to interpret the world: now it is our business to change it." It was to secure that change that their unique partnership had been formed.

Nor was the historical basis of their approach less ample in its survey when they came to write the *Communist Manifesto*. Marx was not merely a philosopher of competence and a jurist of considerable knowledge. He had read widely in German history. He had made a special and profound study of the eighteenth century in France, and, in quite special fullness, of 1789 and its consequences; and, with his usual omnivorous appetite, he had begun those remarkable studies of English economic history and theory which were to culminate, in 1867, in the publication of the first volume of *Capital*. Engels knew the working-class movement in England from the end of the Napoleonic wars in massive detail. He knew the Chartist and trade union movements as one who had not only seen them from the inside, but with a perspective of historical knowledge and insight into contemporary European conditions that were hardly rivalled anywhere at the time. It is, in particular, important to emphasise that, apart from their specialised knowledge, both Marx and Engels, and especially Marx, had an extraordinarily wide general cultivation; each could say, with truth, that *nihil a me alienum putat* had been a choice of inner obligation. They were both polymaths; and one of the striking characteristics they shared, from an early age, was an appreciation of the significance of science in the context of each epoch in which its major developments influence human relations. Few eminent thinkers in social philosophy had, at their age, so superbly prepared themselves for the task which lay to their hand.

# II

The composition of the *Communist Manifesto* is set in the background of the evolution into unity of a number of those groups of exiled revolutionaries which are the inevitable outcome of an age of repression and reaction. Though both the July Revolution of 1830 in France and the abortive Polish rebellion of 1831 had some influence in Germany, neither went deep enough to cause any serious concern. Yet a number of men remained not only profoundly dissatisfied, but eager to continue and further agitation. Among these was a young brush-maker, Johann Philip Becker (1809–84), who saw the need for something more than manifestos and meetings. With great courage, he organised groups of secret conspirators with a view to the prepara-tion of an armed revolution; he himself, indeed, suf-fered imprisonment in 1833, for his activities. These groups were energetic and courageous. They at-tacked prisons, releasing their comrades. They dis-tributed secretly-printed literature. They even attempted to seize the barracks at Frankfurt in order to secure arms. Some of the men who were thus aided to escape from prison, notably Karl Schapper and Theodore Schuster, fled to Paris. There, with other German exiles, they founded in 1833 a secret society to which they gave the name of the Society of the Exiles.

It did not long remain unified. Schuster fell under the influence of Blanqui, then the leading socialist revolutionary in Paris, and his energetic propaganda for Blanquism led to a split in the Society. Schuster and others left it to form a new organisation of their own, which they called the "League of the Just," and this body took part in Blanqui's rising in Paris in 1839. Its members were sent to prison; some of them on their release decided, under the guidance of Schapper, to emigrate to London, where the pol-ice were less hostile to foreigners engaged in political agitation. There they formed a new organisation to which they gave the name—perhaps for purposes of concealment—of the "Workers' Educational Society," in February, 1840. The old "League of the Just" seems simply to have disappeared as a society, and to have survived only in small groups of workers in a number of towns like London, Paris, Brussels and Geneva. Though they became familiar with Left groups in the places to which they emigrated, for the most part they were essentially groups of German exiles, arguing, in the natural fashion of the *émigré*, with ardour and energy among themselves.

One of the best-known members of the "League of the Just" was the German tailor, Wilhelm Weitling, who settled down in Paris in 1837, and became an eager disciple of Blanqui. It was under his influence that Weitling, in 1838, published a defence of revolutionary socialism in the form of a small pamphlet called "Mankind as it is and Ought to be." Involved in Blanqui's rising of 1839, he fled to Switzerland, where he settled down for some years, building up there groups of workers of his turn of mind. In 1842, Weitling published his *Guarantees of Harmony and Freedom*—a book in which his debt to Blanqui is outstanding. He rejected the idea that socialism can be achieved peacefully. He urged the need to provoke revolution; and he argued that the most reliable element upon which the making of a revolution can be built is the *lumpenproletariat*, the casually employed, the homeless, even the criminal classes, who have nothing to lose by participating in the overthrow of the existing order. It is interesting to note that while he was in Switzerland Weitling met Bakunin and was undoubtedly able seriously to influence the ideas of that remarkable Russian personality.

The publication of Weitling's book led to his arrest and imprisonment, together with a number of his comrades, by the Swiss authorities. On his release he was expelled from Switzerland to Germany. There the conspicuous attentions of the police kept him moving from place to place, with the result that he decided, in the early autumn of 1844, to go to London.

His reputation there, even beyond German circles, was already considerable, and a large international gathering was arranged in his honour. Not merely French and German exiles, but English Chartists and trade unionists as well, took part in the celebration. The interest created was sufficient to enable Schapper to found, in October, 1844, "The Society of the Democratic Friends of all Nations," which, it was hoped, would prove a rallying centre for all members of the Left who recognised the need for the revolutionary conquest of political power. Weitling, of course, in the early months of his sojourn in London had great influence in the new organisation. But this did not last long. There were others in the Society, especially Schapper and his friends, who not only knew the English Labour Movement far more fully, and had personal acquaintance with Robert Owen and the trade union leaders, but were deeply hostile to many of Weitling's most cherished ideas. He looked to the poor outcasts of society, and especially to its criminal classes, to be the main architects of the revolution. He saw no special historical significance in the working class as such. Like a good pupil of Blanqui, he thought long-term propaganda and preparation for action largely effort thrown away. He believed in the sudden overthrow

12

of organised government by a surprise attack from a small, but daring, band of reckless revolutionaries. These were at once to inaugurate a Communist order to be governed by a small committee of wise men, somewhat like the Guardians of Plato's *Republic*. To hold the allegiance of the masses, he believed it indispensable for the new government to support religion. Christ was to be proclaimed as the founder of socialism, and the new church would preach a Christianity purified from all dogmas imcompatible with its service to the poor and the suffering.

There is no sort of doubt either in Weitling's ability or of his devotion; Heine's testimony, after meeting him, is sufficient evidence of both. But there is also no doubt that, able though he was, Weitling had little sense of proportion, and that he looked upon criticism as a declaration of enmity. That is shown by his inability to decide whether Communism was more important than the creation of a universal language. Yet, with all his faults and eccentricities, he had made a great impression upon the European socialists. Even before he met Weitling, Marx wrote of his "fiery and brilliant debut"; and he and Engels saw a great deal of him in 1846 when Marx had taken refuge in Brussels after his exile from France. It is also clear that they considered the groups of which Weitling was the intellectual centre as of far more importance than any other, and that they had in mind building a kind of Socialist International around them; Engels tells us that Marx had begun to work out a scheme for a congress of the kind in 1845–46, to be held at Verviers.

But their good relations with, and interest in,

Weitling were of brief duration. They were deeply divided, as Weitling himself tells us, on questions of method. Weitling still insisted that a revolution could be made at any moment, granted resolute leaders, and the skillful use of the *lumpenproletariat*. Marx wished for careful propaganda. He wanted socialists whose character was beyond reproach, and whose theoretical analysis was combined with a real power of agitation and organisation. He was anxious to insist on the folly of any socialist doctrine which evoked the goodwill of the bourgeoisie as a source of change. Since all this was anathema to Weitling, and since, also, he probably resented Marx's challenge to his own leadership, they could not work together; in the spring of 1846 Weitling left Brussels for America. Marx and Engels then devoted themselves to strengthening the Workers' Educational Society. They organised lectures for its members. They formed and kept in close touch with similar groups in London and Paris, as well as in Germany and Switzerland. Even from the incomplete documentation we have, it looks as though Brussels, under Marx, was a kind of central clearing house whence plans for instruction and agitation were initiated. And it looks as though the energy displayed by Marx in this work was the reason why Moll came to him from London, early in 1847, to discuss what was being done by the London committee. It seems, also, that at this meeting it was agreed to call a conference of delegates from the various international committees. This congress met in London in the summer of 1847. Engels represented the Paris Committee, and Wilhelm Wolff, to whom Marx was later to dedicate the first volume of his *Capital*,

represented the Brussels committee. Marx himself
was not present. The handful of delegates founded
the "Communist League" with a provisional constitution which was to be ratified by each of the corresponding committees. It was agreed to issue a
general statement of principles and to publish a popular journal; the London committee even went so far
as to print a trial copy. This is interesting for the attack on the "Utopianism" of Cabet, who was ac-
tively organising his scheme for the foundation of
the socialist colony in America to be called *Icaria* after his well-known book. No other issue of this journal appears to be known.

It is worth while emphasising that, on this view
the Communist League formed in the summer of
1847, was a new central organisation and not, as
Engels has said, merely a continuation of the
League of the Just under another name. This latter
had been, in fact, dissolved by internal schisms; it
had given place to the correspondence committees
mainly organized by Marx, and in a large degree,
directed by him from Brussels. The first conference
of the new League was successful enough to be followed, some months later, by a second conference
which Marx himself attended. He went there with
the knowledge that Engels, the motive force of the
Paris committee, had drawn up the heads of a
"Communist Catechism," though he preferred the
idea of what he called a "Communist Manifesto." At
the second Conference, it seems obvious that Marx
took the lead into his hands and, after stiff and pro-
longed opposition, secured a majority for his proposals, being charged with the task of drawing up a
Manifesto for the League. It also seems clear that, in

some fashion, the London committee became the central organ of the League. This alone explains why, on 26 January, 1848, the London committee could write to the committee in Brussels, enclosing a letter for Marx with a resolution which is nothing less than a command. This resolution must be quoted in full.

"The Central Committee," it runs, "hereby directs the District Committee of Brussels to inform Citizen Marx that if the Manifesto of the Communist Party, which he agreed, at the last congress, to draw up, does not reach London before Tuesday, February 1st, further measures will be taken against him. In the event of Citizen Marx not writing the Manifesto, the Central Committee requests that the documents handed over to him by the Congress shall be returned forthwith. On behalf, and at the instructions of, the Central Committee, Schapper, Bauer, Moll."

From this resolution, certain unmistakable conclusions emerge. It is clear that the Central Committee assumed that Marx was the draftsman of a Manifesto, the lines of which had been agreed upon by the Conference in London in December, 1847. It is clear, further, that documents were entrusted to Marx intended to define the character of the Manifesto. It is clear, moreover, that, so far as the Committee is concerned, the responsibility for drafting the Manifesto was Marx's alone, and it did not regard Engels as either his collaborator or assistant in its composition. This explains the character of the personal letters upon the Manifesto between the two men. Whatever the wishes of the League, they had agreed upon the kind of document they thought necessary; and they decided not to be bound by the instructions Marx had been given by the London Conference. It explains, further, why Engels always insisted that Marx was the major author of the Manifesto, and he himself a minor collaborator in its formulation. It suggests, also, that the London Committee regarded Marx as simply their agent for this purpose, and had the intention, if he did not observe their time-table, of entrusting its composition to someone else; the request for the return of the papers, suggests that, if Marx had not complied with the resolution of 24 January 1848, someone else, probably a member of the League in London, would have been given the task of drafting the Manifesto.

Marx was able to complete his task in time. He must have sent his manuscript to London by 1 February, or shortly thereafter; for it was published in the last days of February. Two things here are of importance. First, the very date of its publication must have meant that it did nothing to precipitate, and had no influence upon, the February Revolution in Paris, which broke out within a few days of the Manifesto's publication in London. Second, it cannot have had any effect on the German risings of that year, since it does not appear to have been known in Germany until at least May, and perhaps June, of 1848. Its main circulation, in the first few months of its existence, was among the members of the Communist League in London and in Brussels. It came to them as a definitive statement of their aims. It was sponsored mainly by Germans, with a sprinkling of Frenchmen, Belgians, and a few members of the Chartist Movement in London. Though its whole tone and outlook was deliberately set in international terms, to most of its readers it must have appeared as essentially related to the conflicts between the socialism of which Marx himself was the chief exponent, with, of course, the indefatigable support of Engels, and that of other groups.

All this is reasonably evident if Engels' own *History of the Communist League* is amended in conjunction with other documents of the time. We know that, on behalf of the London Committee, Schapper and Moll had drawn up an outline of a "Creed" which had been circulated to a few branches and discussed by them. We know, further, that the Paris branch had discussed a draft submitted by the German socialist, Moses Hess; and that Hess's draft was so severely criticised by Engels that the Paris branch asked him to write a new one himself. Engels was elected the Paris delegate to the London Conference of December, 1847, and he made a new draft of his own. In doing so he rejected the term "Creed" and the League's desire for a Catechism by question and answer on the ground that "the statement must contain some history." We have his letter to Marx of 24 November 1847, in which he proposed that "the thing" should be called "Communist Manifesto." He told Marx that his own sketch was "nothing but narrative, and badly flung together, in a frightful hurry." He also urged Marx to "think over the creed a bit." It seems probable that the draft sent by Engels to Marx was largely concerned with the contemporary problems of the international proletariat, and written with a view to being read by working-class readers. If this be correct, Marx must have had before him, in the six or seven weeks during which the *Manifesto* was written, (*a*) a draft from Schapper and Moll, (*b*) the solitary issue of the *Kommunistische Zeitschrift* of September, 1847 where, no doubt at the instance of Engels, the motto of the old League of the Just—"All men are brothers"—had been changed into the historic challenge of "Workers of the World Unite"; (*c*) perhaps, also, the rejected draft of Hess; (*d*) the notes that Engels had made on his way to London. These must have been the papers for the return of which the London Central Committee asked, if Marx did not write the *Manifesto* by 1 February 1848.

In all that he wrote, especially after Marx's death, Engels always insisted that the main ideas of the *Manifesto* came from Marx, and that, both in substance and in composition, it is to Marx that the main credit for it belongs. This is, no doubt, largely true; but we must not make the mistake of underestimating the rôle which, through his natural modesty and generosity, Engels assigned to himself. For, first of all, though the form and style of the *Manifesto* are those of Marx at his most brilliant level, there is a close resemblance between its substance and that of the sketch Engels had made at the desire of the Paris branch of the League. If, moreover, the *Manifesto* is compared with the joint work of the two men, the *German Ideology* (which they wrote between August 1845 and September 1846, and for which they were unable to find a publisher, or with Marx's famous polemic against Proudhin, the *Poverty of Philosophy*, which, though written by Marx alone, drew, with the eager consent of Engels, upon the *German Ideology*) it becomes clear that the two men had, as it were, evolved in common a joint stock of ideas which they regarded as a kind of intellectual bank account upon which

either could draw freely. And even if, on the basis of
Engels' preface to the German edition of 1883,[1]
which is obviously written under the stress of deep
emotion, we grant to Marx all with which Engels so
generously credited him, we must not underestimate
what Marx owed to Engels. It was from Engels that
he learned at first hand how the capitalist system
really works and the significance of Chartism. It was
from Engels that he learned both of the classic English political economy, and of the English socialist
economies developed by men like Hodgskin, Thompson, and Bray, in reply to it. Nor is it unfair to suggest that the inspiration to blend English socialist
economics with the materialist philosophy which the
Left Hegelians had evolved by "standing Hegel on
his head" was the outcome of Engels' inspiration.
And, granted the part that Engels played, both in
the Paris branch of the Communist League, and in
its two London conventions, it is no exaggeration to
say that his skill as a committeeman was largely responsible for getting the first decision of the League
to assign the task of actually drafting the *Manifesto*
to Marx. No one realised more clearly than Engels
that once in Marx's hands it would become a good
deal more than an appeal from a small organisation
with less than a thousand members; it would be a
call to action from the vanguard of a working class
which, over large areas of Europe, was just about to
embark upon an attempt at large-scale revolution.

One or two other minor points may be made. The
*Manifesto* was published in London at the end of
February, 1848. It began serial publication in the

[1] The preface is dated 28 June; Marx died on 14 March, 1883.

*Deutsche Londoner Zeitung,* the little journal of the German *émigrés* in England, on 3 March. On 4 March, the Belgian police expelled Marx. Returning to Paris within the next week he met Schapper, Bauer and Moll from the London Germans, and George Julian Harney and Ernest Jones from the English Chartists, to concert joint plans; it was agreed, as Marx wrote to Engels, that the Central Committee of the League should be moved to Paris, with Marx as its President. A large number of copies of the *Manifesto,* perhaps one thousand, reached Paris about 20 March; and it was beginning to arrive in Germany early in April. In the *Preface* to the German edition of 1872, Marx and Engels tell us that the French translation first appeared in Paris before the June days of 1848, and that the first English translation, made by Helen Macfarlane, appeared in Harney's *Red Republican* in 1850; it ran through four numbers of November in that year. In the edition of 1872 Marx and Engels tell us that a Polish version appeared in London shortly after the original edition, as did also a Danish translation. A Russian edition, translated by Bakunin, was published in the earlier sixties; a revised version, translated by Plekhanov, though in his special preface to the German edition of 1890, Engels attributes it to Vera Zasulitch, was published in 1882. In 1888, a revised English translation was made by Engels' friend, Samuel Moore, and edited with notes of his own by Engels himself; it was published by the well-known Socialist, William Reeves. The first American translation appears to have been published in 1872 in *Woodhull and Chaplin's Weekly;* it may well be that these two well-known radical feminists published it on account of the removal of the head-quarters of the International to New York in that year, as a result of the internal struggles between Marxists and the followers both of Proudhon and Bakunin. At the present time it exists in practically every written language of importance all over the world.

It is worth noting the character of the relations between Marx and Engels and the English working-class movement before the publication of the *Manifesto*. The contact was first made personally by Engels when the latter was writing his *Condition of the Working Class in England* in 1843. Through Mary Burns, with whom he began to live soon after his first arrival in Manchester, he met John Watson, a socialist tailor, who was a leading figure there among the Owenites, and James Leach, a man of ability and character who was among the outstanding Chartists in Manchester. In the summer of 1843 Engels went to Leeds, primarily to meet George Julian Harney, then virtually the editor of the *Northern Star*. Engels made a vivid impression on Harney and they remained friends until the former's death; it is not unlikely that it was through this friendship that Harney became, with the exception of Bronterre O'Brien, one of the few English social-ists before the foundation of the *International* who had knowledge of, and interest in, the socialist movements in Europe. It was perhaps through these connections that Engels began to write, in the Labour press, articles intended to explain, and arouse interest in, the revolutionary movements abroad. In November 1843, in the Owenite *New Moral World* he published an admirable article on the *Advance of*

*Social Reform on the Continent.* There he sought to show that, even if there were differences of approach, there was bound to be the overthrow of capitalism in England, France and Germany. There might be divergent opinions from time to time; but it was urgent for the different movements to be in touch with each other. After his return to Germany, he wrote in December, 1844, a second article in the same journal called *The Swift Progress of Communism in Germany.* At this stage, he was still arguing, influenced perhaps by his then close relations with Moses Hess, that the intelligentsia would be the makers of the German revolution. Certainly, he had found it difficult, in the police-state that Germany was then, to find ways and means of exercising any influence on the workers.

Engels returned to England in the summer of 1845, with Marx as his companion. They stayed for several weeks, visiting Manchester as well as London, and it was then that Engels became a fairly regular contributor to the *Northern Star* and began to insist that the working class alone could achieve its own salvation by breaking the power of the bourgeoisie. During this visit, also, William Lovett, at the instance of Karl Schapper, appealed to Chartists to join the London branch of the Workers' Educational Society. There was a fair response to his appeal; among those who joined were Harney, Ernest Jones and Thomas Cooper. Thenceforward the *Northern Star* began to publish reports of the meetings and lectures of the German socialists, and to pay a good deal more attention to the European movement. In the *Northern Star* of 25 July 1846, there is a letter in its pages, signed by Marx, Engels and Gisot, on behalf of the German branch in Brussels, which congratulates Feargus O'Connor for standing as a Chartist candidate for Nottingham. The letter praises the paper for its insight into English politics; it points out that, as O'Connor and the *Northern Star* have clearly seen, the real struggle in England is between the middle class and the workers, between capital and labour.

There was now a constant, if fragile, relation between Chartism and continental socialism through the medium of the Communist League. At the November Congress of the League, in 1847, an international meeting was held, at which both Marx and Engels were present, to celebrate the anniversary of the Polish rebellion of 1830. Harney, Ernest Jones and Kydd, the author of the *History of the Factory Laws*, were the English speakers; Marx and Engels were among the foreign guests who spoke. We have a report of Marx's speech in the *Northern Star* of 4 December 1847. "I have been sent by the Brussels Democrats," he said, "to speak with the Democrats of London to call on them to cause to be holden a Congress of Nations—a Congress of Working Men, to establish liberty all over the world. The middle classes, the free traders, held a congress in Brussels, but their fraternity is one-sided, and the moment that such congresses are likely to benefit the working man, that moment their fraternity will cease and their congresses dissolve. The Democrats of Belgium and the Chartists of England are the real democrats, and the moment they carry the six points of their Charter, the road to liberty will be opened to the world. Effect this grand object, you workmen of England, and you will be hailed as the saviours of

the whole human race." The speech is, no doubt,
one of Marx's polite expressions of international
working-class fraternity to which delegates give expression at meetings of this kind; but it has a special
interest from the fact that the Marx who spoke it
was returning directly to Brussels, charged by the
Communist League with the task of drawing up that
Manifesto which was to be a challenge to more than
a century of subsequent history.

# III

The *Communist Manifesto* has passed beyond the
stage where it requires any eulogy. It is admitted by
every serious student of society to be one of the outstanding political documents of all time; in the influence it has exerted it compares with the American
Declaration of Independence of 1776, and the
French Declaration of Rights of 1789. Its character
is unique, not only because of the power with which
it is written, but also because of the immense scope
it covers in its intense brevity. It is a philosophy of
history, a critical analysis of socialist doctrines and a
passionate call to revolutionary action. In each of
these phases, it is written as a deliberate and provoc-
ative challenge. Its aim is to make the working class
conscious of a great historical mission, and to com-
municate to it the deep sense of urgency about that
mission which Marx and Engels themselves
possessed. Its savage invective is intended to strip

the veil from those bourgeois foundations of the existing order the concealment of which is one of the ways in which capitalist civilisation hides its real purposes from the workers whom it makes its slaves. But its invective is intended also to safeguard the workers from being deceived by other doctrines, claiming to be socialist, which, in the judgment of Marx and Engels, are intended to turn the workers from their vital task of abolishing a society built on the exploitation of one class by another and so building the classless society. The *Manifesto*, it must be added, is a remarkable feat of compression; and though its ringing sentences make it, on a first reading, seem simple and straightforward, there are, in fact, behind almost every phase of it the marks of profound intellectual conflict, without the grasp of which the reader is only too likely to miss both the decisiveness of the document and its great complexity. For one of the purposes of the *Manifesto* is the definition of a doctrine which, though rooted in the massive discussions which had taken place ever since the conspiracy of Babeuf and, in particular, since the French Revolution of 1830, was intended to supersede all competing theories, and thus to unify a chaos of ideas into a philosophy which bound the workers together and prepared the basis of action.

The originality of the *Manifesto* does not lie in any single doctrine that it enunciates. It draws upon an immense body of literature, not all of it socialist, in which a number of the doctrines which lie at the heart of classical Marxism had already been set out with clarity and with vigour. Its originality lies in the skill, first of all, with which these doctrines are

woven together so as to form a logical whole; and,
second, in putting in the perspective of ultimate
revolutionary prophecy the outlines of an immediate
programme so conceived as to be directly related to
the demands of the workers in the major European
countries, as these had been born out of their practical experience of capitalist domination. Two other
things, moreover, must be said. It is evident from the
whole content of the *Manifesto* that when it was
written both Marx and Engels were convinced that
the day of reckoning was close at hand, and this was
why there was a certain apocalyptic note of urgency
about their discussions. It is not less evident that
they believed—of course quite mistakenly—that the
birthplace of the social revolution they anticipated
was certain to be Germany. No one can seriously
doubt that they had immensely overestimated the
degree to which revolutionary socialist ideas had
penetrated the German working class; and brave as
was the fight they put up in particular places, remarkable as was the literature they published in
their cause, their enthusiasm allotted to the German
movement a priority it was far from ready to assume. On any detached analysis the France of
1848 was, alike in ideas and in action, far more
mature than the Germany of the same years; it is impossible not to feel that this emerges in Marx's own
two classic pamphlets, *The Eighteenth Brumaire of
Louis Napoleon* (1852) and the *Class Struggles in
France* (1850). Anyone who compares these with
his account of the German struggles of the same
years, cannot fail to note what it is difficult not to
call an almost Utopian element in his description of
German events and their implications. They pitched

their expectations of the outcome of the German Revolt unjustifiably high; they tended to exaggerate both the influence and the significance of their own supporters. It may even be doubted whether they fully realised how deep were the internal divisions in the movement they sought to lead; or how difficult was the achievement of that democratic centralism which the *Manifesto* put forward as the basis of organised proletarian action.

It is, moreover, obvious, both from their references to the Owenite movement and to Chartism, that, though Marx and Engels were aware of important trends in English thought, they tended to underestimate their significance both for doctrine and for action. Even though Engels' studies had since 1842 brought him into close contact with the English workers' movement, it is doubtful if at this stage he fully understood its possibilities; Marx who, apart from two brief visits to England in 1845 and 1847, knew only of the British movement at second hand from Engels, had hardly begun those massive studies of English political activity and theory which, in the *Critique of Political Economy* (1859) and the first volume of *Capital* (1867), were to bear such remarkable fruit. It was not until they had both settled down in England, after the failure of revolution in France and Germany, that they really began to grasp the full importance of an English tradition which not only bourgeois economists like Sir William Petty, Adam Smith, Malthus and Ricardo had their share in making, but in which that classical tradition had been challenged by Owen and his followers, by Hodgskin and Bray; only then did they understand how much more was to be gained from a full study of the English scene than from that of France or of Germany. Here, they began to see, was already the most mature expression of capitalism's habits; and they could only prophesy its outcome by the careful and detailed study of its operation. But, by that time, the *Communist Manifesto* had already taken a dogmatic position in their thinking; and their tendency, henceforward, was to judge the English movement less by the scene which unfolded itself before their eyes, than by the degree to which they could fit its postulates of action into those they had so stoutly defended in the *Manifesto*. In the early years of their exile, they assumed that the habits of the English trade union movement were due to their theoretical backwardness; they awoke with relative slowness to its significance alongside the magnificent slogans with which the French and German workers were accustomed to decorate their doctrines. It was not until both men had realised that the English movement was to be the context in which the major part of their lives was likely to be passed that they gave it the full consideration it deserved. Even then, when they could desert its analysis for the large-scale *Weltanschauung* of some German or French doctrinaire, they continued to feel far more at home in socialist exegesis. However much Engels made himself at home with English habits it is important to remember that Marx was always a German who lived, very consciously, *in partibus infidelium*, and was never able to alter the categories of his thinking from those of his native land. Engels, for him, was always a remarkable source of fertile English illustration; the core of Marx's approach was Franco-German experience.

Late in life, he realised the significance of Russia; but England was an illustration of a thesis in the main largely formed when he first entered the library of the British Museum.

# IV

The actual construction of the *Communist Manifesto* is brilliantly simple. Affirming, with justice, the dread of communism felt by the governments of Europe, it goes on to insist that the struggle between classes is the central clue to historical change. But whereas in previous periods the structure of society is a "complicated arrangement," in the new "epoch of the bourgeoisie" society is being ever more "simplified" by being forced towards the dual division between bourgeoisie and proletariat. The *Manifesto* emphasises the revolutionary part the bourgeoisie has played in history, its relentless drive to make the "cash nexus" the only bond between men. It has dissolved innumerable other freedoms for the one freedom which gives it command of the world market—freedom of trade. It lives by exploitation, and its unresting search for markets means an unending and profound change in every aspect of life. It gives a "cosmopolitan character to production and consumption in every country." It compels the breakdown of national isolation; as it builds an inter-dependent material universe, so it draws, as a common fund, upon science and learning from every nation. It means the centralisation of government, the supremacy of town over country, the dependence of backward peoples upon those with more advanced methods of production in their hands.

The *Manifesto* describes with savage eloquence how the development of bourgeois society makes the workman a wage-slave exploited by the capitalist. The latter spares neither age nor sex. He makes it increasingly impossible for the small producer to compete with him; on every side economic power is increasingly concentrated and the little man, in every category of industry and agriculture, is driven into the dependent condition of the working class. So ruthless is this exploitation that in sheer self-defence the workers are compelled to combine to fight their masters. They form unions, ever more wide, which come at last to fight together as a class and as a political party representative of that class. If the battle sways backwards and forwards, with gains here and losses there, the consolidation of the workers as a class hostile to their exploiters has one special feature which distinguishes it from all previous struggles between rulers and ruled; the working class becomes increasingly the self-conscious, independent movement of the immense majority, in the interest of the immense majority. If at first it struggles within the framework of the national state, it soon becomes evident that this struggle is but one act in a vast international drama. A time comes in the history of capitalism when "its existence is no longer compatible with society." It cannot feed its slaves. It drives them to revolution in which a proletarian victory is inevitable.

The *Manifesto* then turns to the special functions

of Communists in the working-class movement. It insists that the Communists do not form "a separate party opposed to other working-class parties." They have no interest apart from the workers. More than this: "They do not set up any sectarian principles of their own," says the *Manifesto*, "by which to mould and shape the proletarian movement." Their task is to insist on the international solidarity of the working class, to stand in its vanguard in each country, to aid, by their deeper theoretical grasp of the movement of history, in the workers' drive to the conquest of power. They do not aim at the abolition of individual private property, but of that bourgeois form of the ownership of the instruments of production which deprives nine-tenths of society of the capacity to acquire individual property. Communists admit freely that they desire to abolish the bourgeois corruption of the family and to replace home education by social education. They do so because the bourgeois family is a means of exploiting the labour of women and children, and because bourgeois education means its subordination to the ends of the ruling class. If Communists are charged with seeking to abolish love of country, the *Manifesto* answers that the workers can have no country until they are emancipated from bourgeois domination; with their acquisition of political power, the hostility between nations will disappear. So, also, it will change traditional ideas in religion and philosophy. Since it puts experience on a new basis, it will change the ideas which are their expression.

The *Manifesto* recognises that the emancipation of the workers will never come in exactly the same way in every country; differences in development

make that inevitable. Yet it suggests a programme of
measures, "generally applicable" in advanced countries, which will enable the workers to win the battle
of democracy. When this victory has been won, under these conditions class distinctions will disappear
and the state-power will wither away, since it is
necessary only to preserve class-distinctions. In its
place there will be a free association of citizens "in
which the free development of each will be the condition of the free development of all."

Such a summary as this, of course, is bound to do
injustice to the superb sweep of the *Manifesto* itself.
But it is important to dwell upon it for the implications upon which it insists. First, perhaps, a word is
useful on the title of the document itself. It was to
have been the "Catechism" by way of question and
answer, from the Communist League; it became the
*Communist Manifesto*. What is the reason for the
change? Partly, no doubt, the decision of Marx and
Engels to alter what would have been an essentially
temporary domestic piece of propaganda into one
that would have permanent historical value. It is
hard not to believe that they called it a *Manifesto* in
tribute to the memory of the Babouviste *Manifesto
of the Equals*. They always recognised Babeuf as a
real precursor, and do honour to him in their own
work. The word *Communist*, it may fairly be suggested, has a double implication. On the one hand,
it emphasises the relation of their work to the Communist League, by which they were authorised to
undertake it; on the other, it serves to mark their
own sense of profound separation from the "true" socialists of Germany, and especially of Karl Grün,
against whom their criticism was so evident in the

*Manifesto* itself. They reproached "true" socialism with sentimentality, with pretentiousness, and with an abstract approach to concrete problems which deprived them of any sense of reality. One can already see the depth of their hostility to Grün in articles they had written against him in August and September, 1847.[1] It would not be surprising that they should choose a title for their pronouncements which at once looked back to a great revolutionary predecessor, and avoided the danger of any confusion with a group whose "socialism" seemed to them no more than a vapid humanitarianism.

What lends support to this view is the emphatic declaration of Marx and Engels that the Communists do not form a separate party. On the contrary, they are ready to work with all working-class organisations genuinely dedicated to the socialist task; more, they repudiate any claim to "sectarian" doctrines of their own which might result in their separation from the rest of the working-class movement. It is vital to insist upon this emphasis. However critical Marx and Engels may be of other socialist principles than their own, their regard for unity among the working-class forces is paramount. That is shown by their careers from the very outset. Engels lent his support to Chartism even before the appearance of the *Manifesto;* yet there must have been few among its leaders who had any real insight into the doctrines of which he was the exponent. He and Marx were often bitterly hostile to the German Social Democratic Movement; they attacked Lassalle, Lieb-

---

[1] They were originally printed in the *Westphalische Dampfboot;* they were reprinted in the *Neue Zeit* for 1895–6 (vol. I, pp. 51 et seq.).

knecht, Bebel, Kautsky. But they never sought to found a separate German Communist Party. The hostility of Marx to the dominant elements in French socialism is obvious from his attack on Proudhon as early as 1847; but though he and Engels always encouraged the "Marxist" elements in the French party, the *Civil War in France* (1871) of Marx himself shows their anxiety to assist it, even when they thought its policy mistaken. Indeed, Section IV of the *Manifesto* itself insists upon this view. The Communists support the Chartists in England and the Agrarian Reformers in America; they "ally themselves" with the Social Democratic Party in France; they support the radicals in Switzerland, "without forgetting that the party consists of contradictory elements"; in Poland they support "the party that has seen in an agrarian revolution the means to national freedom, that party which caused the insurrection of Cracow in 1846"; in Germany they fight with any bourgeois elements which see the need to "act in a revolutionary manner against the absolute monarchy, the feudal landlords, and the little middle class."

The *Manifesto*, without question, insists that the Communists enter into relations with other groups to give them direction, to spread their own revolutionary creed, to make the workers aware of the "hostile antagonism" between bourgeoisie and proletariat. They "openly declare that their ends can be attained only by the forcible overthrow of all existing social conditions." But this declaration follows upon the announcement of three purposes which must be kept closely in mind if it is to be fully understood. They support "every revolutionary movement against the existing social and political order of things." In every movement, moreover, whatever its stage of development, they put the question of property in the first place. "Equally," says the *Manifesto,* "they labour everywhere for the union and agreement of the democratic parties of all countries."

If all this is read in the context of Engels' famous introduction to Marx's *Class Struggles in France,*[1] which he wrote in 1895, and of the joint *Address of the Central Council of the Communist League,*[2] it is clear that the *Manifesto* is presenting a doctrine of permanent revolution. By that famous phrase they do not mean a continuous series of attempts to seize the state-power by the workers in the manner advocated by Blanqui. They had learned that revolution was an art, and that it needs certain special historical conditions if it is to be successful. They meant that when an alliance of the progressive forces in society overthrows the reactionary forces, the workers must not allow bourgeois democrats or social reformers to stop at the point where private ownership of the means of production remains unchallenged. They must always drive them on from this reformist outlook to the revolutionary stage where direct attack is made on private property. Even if the conditions do not permit of success, at least they will have done much to educate those workers who are not yet class-conscious into a realisation of their position. And, with the coming of universal suffrage, the revo-

---

[1] I use the full text as published in *Selected Works of Karl Marx* (Moscow, 1935), vol. II, p. 169. Marx's analysis originally appeared in the *Neue Rheinische Zeitung* from March to June, 1850.
[2] It was written at the end of March, 1850.

lutionary idea will, by force of historical circumstances, enable the Communists to "conquer the
greater part of the middle section of society, petty
bourgeois and small peasants, and grow into the decisive power in the land, before which all other powers will have to bow, whether they like it or not. To
keep this growth going without interruption, until of
itself it gets beyond the control of the ruling govern-
mental system, not to fritter away this daily increas-
ing shock force in advance guard fighting, but to
keep it intact until the day of the decision—that is
our main task."[1]

The continuation is not less significant. "The irony
of world history," wrote Engels, "turns everything
upside down. We, 'the revolutionaries,' the 'rebels,'
we are thriving far better on legal methods than on
illegal methods and revolt . . . The parties of order, as they call themselves, are perishing under the
legal conditions created by themselves . . . and if
we are not so crazy as to let ourselves be driven into
street fighting in order to please them, then nothing
else is finally left for them but to break through this
legality so fatal to them."[2] Nothing here written by
Engels means that he assumed the likelihood that
the final transition from capitalism to socialism
would be peaceful. On the contrary, it is quite evident that he expected the peaceful forces of socialism so to develop that their strength became a threat
to the interests of property. That threat, he pro-
phesied, would lead the interests of property themselves to break the Constitution. Where that occurred Social Democracy would then be free to act

[1] Engels, op. cit., vol. II, p. 189.
[2] Ibid.

in its own defence. That, for him, is the moment when a revolutionary struggle would begin. He did not neglect the danger that progress towards socialism might be halted by war on a global scale. "No war is any longer possible for Prussia-Germany," he wrote,[1] "except a world war, and a world war indeed of an extension and violence hitherto undreamed of. Eight to ten millions of soldiers will mutually massacre one another and, in doing so, devour the whole of Europe until they have stripped it barer than any swarm of locusts has ever done. The devastations of the Thirty Years' War compressed into three or four years; and spread over the whole Continent; famine, pestilence, general demoralisation both of the armies and of the mass of the people produced by acute distress; hopeless confusion of our artificial machinery in trade, industry and credit, ending in general bankruptcy; collapse of the old states and their traditional state-wisdom to such an extent that crowns will roll by dozens on the pavement, and there will be no one to pick them up; absolute impossibility of foreseeing how it will end, and who will come out of the struggle as victor; only one result is absolutely certain: general exhaustion, and the establishment of the conditions for the ultimate victory of the working class. This is the prospect when the system of mutual outbidding in armaments, driven to extremities, at last bears its inevitable fruits. This, my lords and gentlemen, is where, in your wisdom, you have brought old Eu-

[1] Preface to Borkheim's *In Memory of the German Martyrs who died for their Fatherland 1806–1807*, quoted in *Correspondence of Marx and Engels* (London, 1934), p. 456. Cf. also ibid. p. 429, 455.

rope. And when nothing more remains to you but to open the last great war dance—that will suit us all right. The war may perhaps push us temporarily into the background, may wrench from us many a position already conquered. But when you have un-fettered forces which you will then no longer be able again to control, things may go as they will; at the end of the tragedy you will be ruined, and the victory of the proletariat will either be already achieved, or, at any rate, inevitable." Nor does he fail to note, in a letter to Sorge, of 7 January 1888, that "American industry would conquer all along the line, and push us up against the alternatives: either retrogression to production for home consumption . . . or—social transformation . . . but once the first shot is fired, control ceases, the horse can take the bit between his teeth."[1]

To this should be added what Marx and Engels had to say in the edition, prepared by the latter, of Marx's famous address to the General Council of the First International on the Civil War in France which arose out of the defeat of Louis Napoleon in the Franco-Prussian War. "In reality," wrote Engels, in his preface of 18 March 1871,[2] "the state is noth-ing but a machine for the oppression of one class by another, and, indeed, in the democratic republic, no less than in the monarchy; and, at best, an evil in-herited by the proletariat after its victorious struggle for class supremacy, whose worst sides, the pro-letariat, just like the Commune, cannot avoid leav-

[1] Preface to Borkheim's *In Memory of the German Martyrs who died for their Fatherland* 1806–1807, quoted in *Correspondence of Marx and Engels* (London, 1934), p. 456, and pp. 489–91.
[2] *Selected Works*, vol. II, p. 460.

ing to lop off until such time, at the earliest possible moment, as a new generation, reared in new and free social conditions, will be able to throw the entire lumber of the state on the scrap-heap. Of late, the Social Democratic philistine has once more been filled with terror at the words: dictatorship of the proletariat. Well and good, gentlemen, do you want to know what this Dictatorship looks like? Look at the Paris Commune. That was the Doctatorship of the Proletariat!"

No one can examine this section of the *Manifesto* honestly without coming to two conclusions, especially when it is set in the light of the subsequent comments upon its meaning by its own authors. They did not expect that capitalist society would be transformed into socialist society without violent revolution. They were insistent that the people who shared their views must never divide the organised working-class forces, that it was their duty to avoid sectarianism, and that they must not form a separate party. Their task was to be the vanguard of their party, to proclaim, indeed, their views, to do all in their power to get them accepted as the basis of action, but still to remain within the political ranks of the organised working class. More than this: in the last edition of the *Manifesto* edited by Engels, though he remained emphatic in his belief that violence would accompany the final disappearance of capitalism, he was also emphatic that the workers would be foolish to rely upon the old methods of street-fighting at the barricades, because new methods and new weapons had altered the situation in favour of the armed forces and the police. Fighting might still be necessary, but it would be folly for the workers to abandon legal methods until a stage had been reached when the position they confronted compensated for the new strength a capitalist society possessed in the power at the disposal of the state authority.

Under what circumstances did the workers reach that position? The answer, surely, is given by the fact that Marx saw the dictatorship of the proletariat as the outcome of the Paris Commune when France was defeated by Prussia in the war of 1870. Engels saw it, as is evident from the preface of 1895 to the *Manifesto*, and from his introduction to Borkheim's book, as the outcome of the catastrophic conditions produced by global war. It is of decisive importance to consider these views in the light of the interpretation that Lenin himself put upon them. He pointed out, with perfect fairness, the immense step taken by Marx between the publication of the *Manifesto* and the *Eighteenth Brumaire*,[1] and between these pamphlets and both the *Letters to Kugelmann* and the *Civil War in France*,[2] he draws attention, too, again quite fairly, to a similar charge in the outlook of Engels between the production of the *Manifesto* and the careful analysis of the *Anti-Dühring*;[3] but the vital outlook of Lenin is set out in his classic *State and Revolution* and the documents therewith connected. It is sufficient here to say that Lenin was here concerned to establish to the comrades in Leningrad the necessary conditions of successful revolution; for he, like Marx and Engels, was careful to distinguish his

[1] *The State and Revolution* in *Select Works* (London, 1937), vol. VII, p. 5.
[2] Letter of 12 April, 1871, and cf. Lenin, op. cit., p. 27.
[3] Ibid., p. 16.

outlook from that of Blanqui. He thought it necessary, first, that the armed forces of the state-power
should be disloyal. He thought that the machinery of the state must be in ruins; there must be
widespread revolutionary disturbance among the
working class, as evidenced by strikes and dem-
onstrations and there must be a solid and coher-
ent working-class power able to lead the working
class to the conquest of power. On these conditions,
working-class victory was a possibility with a real
prospect of success. Here, it will be noted that Lenin
is considering a condition in which the overwhelm-
ing breakdown of the machinery of government
opened the prospect of new orientations.[1] The
breakdown of ancient state-powers as the outcome of
the war of 1939 had resulted in something akin to
that which Lenin had foreseen. That was the result
of defeat in war. The form of state has remained
unaltered in the states which remained victorious in
that struggle. Lenin was pretty clearly right in insist-
ing that the "democratic republic," based on universal suffrage, was the last rampart of bourgeois
socialism rather than the first of democratic socialism in the Marxian sense of that term; that can be
seen from utterances like those of Macaulay and of
Daniel Webster. But nothing in his discussion deals
with the fundamental point of whether and why
that extreme Left he represented was justified in dis-
senting from the continuous insistence of Marx and

[1] As is made clear in the preface to the first edition of the *State
and Revolution*. "An international proletarian revolution," Lenin
writes, "is clearly maturing. The question of its relation to the state
is acquiring practical importance."

Engels that the working class opposed to the imposition of bourgeois capitalism should form a separate party from the old social democrats. In this regard, the famous split between Bolsheviks and Mensheviks, at the Congress in London in 1903, was an innovation unconsidered by his predecessors. Whether it was wise or unwise, together with all the immense consequences to which, since the foundation of the Third International in 1919, it has led, lies outside the scope of this introduction.

# V

From this remarkable analysis, the *Manifesto* goes on a little cursorily and haphazardly, to consider the literature of socialism which had appeared up to 1848. It condemns, first of all, what it calls "reactionary" socialism as a form of capitalism the roots of which lie deep in a feudal outlook. It seems probable that the author had in mind, without naming them, two groups of thinkers. On the one hand they were attacking the attempts of men like Herman Wagener and Bismarck who were seeking an alliance between the Prussian Crown and the proletariat, primarily at the expense, immediately, of the bourgeoisie, but ultimately, of the proletariat. These were seeking, in the old technique, how first to divide in order that their royal master might govern without question. They were in all probability

attacking also the *soi-disant* socialism of Louis Rous-
seau and Villeneuve-Bargemont in France, who
sought, by putting the French unemployed into agricultural colonies, to prevent them from strengthening the army of the proletariat by leaving the
supporters of the "juste milieu" face to face with
their bourgeoisie. Above all, they were dismissing
that "Young England" group, of which Disraeli, as
in *Sybil*, with some support from George Smythe
and, at a remoter distance, Thomas Carlyle, supplied the ideas, and for which Lord John Manners
provided, with occasional support from Lord Ashley
(the later Earl of Shaftesbury), the political leadership. They, together with the Christian Socialists, of
whom F. D. Maurice and Charles Kingsley were the
outstanding figures, were groups of which Engels,
with his accustomed prescience, had already seen
the danger in his *Condition of the Working Class in
England in 1844*.

Engels, at least, had not failed to understand the
importance of Carlyle's *Chartism* (1840) and of his
*Past and Present* (1843); he had already written
about them in the *Deutsch-französische Jahrbücher.*[1]
He had fully understood the reality of their hor-
ror of the new factory system, the new poor law,
the invasion of happy lives by the new and grim
industrialism. But the *Manifesto* regarded this
type of socialism as no more than feudalism,
however much its plea might be garbed in eloquence. Marx saw that they loathed the effects of industrialism; but he realised that they wanted to go

[1] Paris, 1844, pp. 152–81.

44

backwards to a paternalistic feudalism, not forward to a democratic socialism. They were afraid of a rebellion from the oppressed, and they hoped to buy it off by paternal concessions which would still leave Tory Democracy in power. Since this was in its essence aristocratic and would, as in the Ten Hours Bill, improve factory conditions without removing the indignity of an unemancipated class, the *Manifesto* rejects this attempt to return to "Merrie England" as an effort without serious meaning for socialists who had really grasped the problem before the proletariat.

They then turned to the analysis of petty-bourgeois socialism. The *Manifesto* admits freely the achievements of this school of doctrine, at the head of which, both for France and England, it places the distinguished name of Sismondi. But it argues that, apart from its important criticism of modern production, the petty-bourgeois school has no positive aim but to restore "the old property relations, and the old society." It is therefore dismissed as both "reactionary and utopian"; "this form of socialism," says the *Manifesto*, "ended in a miserable fit of the blues."

This is far from being a fair picture. It is true enough that Sismondi announced his hopeless sense of bankruptcy before the results of the new system of production, the outcome of which he described so well. But it is curious that there is no tribute to French writers like Buret—to whom Engels owed a special debt—and Vidal, still less to Constantin Pecquer, who had the keen insight to see that the *petit bourgeois* is part of a numerous class which forms, as it were, the rag-bag into which are thrown both bankrupt peasants and outmoded craftsmen.[1] Nor is it fair to the remarkable English school, like Hodgskin and Thompson and Bray, some knowledge of whom it is difficult to suppose was absent from men as eagerly interested in Chartism as Marx and Engels. It may be that the abrupt brevity with which the "petty bourgeois school" is dismissed is partly due to their failure to depict the revolution, the coming of which is, of course, the main prophecy of the *Manifesto;* this leads naturally into the bitter attack that is made, in the next section, on "true" or German socialism.

This attack may be regarded as the final breach of Marx and Engels with that Hegelian Left to which both of them had once belonged. It is the demonstration not only that its leaders were living by concepts and not by things, but also that the result of their effort was merely to serve the ends of German reaction. It is here that Marx and Engels break with their own past. They have done with Ruge and Moses Hess, with Karl Grün and Hermann Kriege. The stride beyond Hegel which Feuerbach had taken, which was in large part the basis of "true" socialism, now is declared not only inadequate but also deceptive. The votaries of "true" socialism are using the great principles of revolutionary experience and thought in France to elucidate a situation to which they are inapplicable. They fail to see that French socialism is an attack upon a bourgeoisie already in power. In Germany this is not the case. There the bourgeoisie has only begun to fight

[1] C. Pecquer, *Des Intérêts du Commerce* (1844), vol. II, pp. 208–9.

against the feudal aristocracy. To fight for socialism under these conditions is to delay the success of the bourgeois revolution by frightening it with the threat of a proletarian attack for which the conditions are completely unripe. "True" socialism, the *Manifesto* argues, thus "served the governments (of Germany) as a weapon for fighting the German bourgeoisie." It thus delays the march of the necessary historical development by serving up as "eternal truths" concepts the value of which depends wholly upon their relevance to the concrete situation. The "true" socialists are thus guilty of an abstract philosophy which appears like a call to arms; but it is a call which can have no other result than to aid the victory of feudal reaction by seeking a revolutionary temper in a class which has not yet decisively appeared upon the historic stage.

That Marx and Engels were wholly right in their attitude to "true" socialism was shown conclusively by the events of 1848 in Germany. There is indeed an important sense in which their criticism of German socialism has remained valid right down to our own time. The "true" socialists, as they said, borrowed the formulae of French socialism. They then not merely refrained from universalising them. What was worse, they made their realisation seem a special German mission, the task to be accomplished by a German nation which was a "model" nation, by a German "petty philistine" whom they looked upon as the "typical man." It is a high tribute to the insight of Marx and Engels that they had thus perceived what, indeed, they had begun to realise as early as 1845, that "true" socialism was deeply infected with the taint of German romanticism; and that this, in its nationalist form, gave to the socialist expression of its ideals the same arrogant sense of a superior place in the fulfilment of their purpose as, upon another plane of thought, Fichte and Hegel gave to Germany as a compensation for its humiliation by Napoleon. When Hess call the German people the nation "at once the most universal and the most European," he was claiming for it the same supreme place in the hierarchy of socialist effort as was Hegel when he made the Prussian monarchy coincide with the ultimate purpose of the absolute. It was an analogous reliance upon what the *Manifesto* calls "speculative cobwebs embroidered with flowers of rhetoric" which made German socialism in 1914 so overwhelmingly take up arms in an imperialist war and in 1918–19, by manipulating concepts instead of realities, rejoice, as the Weimer Republic was built, in the success of a revolution that had not yet happened. There is no part of the *Manifesto* more rich in understanding than the bitter paragraphs in which Marx and Engels so severely attack men with whom, but recently, they had been in close alliance. Nor should we omit to note the important sense in which this criticism is as much directed against an earlier phase of their own thinking at it is against their friends. It is because Hess and Grün had failed to see that the idealist methodology, of Hegel, and even of Feuerbach, could never be the basis of an effective socialist movement, that they were handled with so determined a severity.

The section on literature continues with a discussion of "conservative or bourgeois" socialism. "The socialistic bourgeois," says the *Manifesto,* "want all

the advantages of modern social conditions without
the struggles and dangers necessarily resulting from
them. They desire the present state of society without its revolutionary and disintegrating elements.
They wish for a bourgeoisie without a proletariat."
The "conservative" socialist may be an economist or
a humanitarian; he is found among "hole and corner
reformers of every kind." If he systematises his doctrine, he emerges with a body of ideas like those ex-
pounded by Proudhon in his *Philosophie de la
Misère*. Or he may refrain from system-making,
and devote his attention to attacks on revolutionary
movements intended to persuade the workers of
their folly. Political reform will not do. Nor is anything gained by abolishing the bourgeois relations of
production. In the eyes of the "conservative" socialist the supreme need is a change in "the material
conditions of existence." When we analyse what he
means by this change, we find that it is no more
than "administrative reforms" which, though they
simplify the work and diminish the cost of government, leave the relations between capital and labour
unchanged. He is in favour of free trade, or protective duties, or prison reform, for the benefit of the
working class. What, nevertheless, is vital to his outlook is that the proletariat should cease to hate the
bourgeoisie, and accept the capitalist system as final.
By that means the "social New Jerusalem" can be
built without the haunting fear that revolution is
necessary to its establishment.

It is obvious enough that this attack is directed
against the men whose palliatives Marx agreed with
Proudhon in dismissing with contempt in his *Poverty of Philosophy*—Proudhon himself, be it noted,

being added by Marx to the list of those to be so dismissed. Michel Chevalier, Adolphe Blanqui and Léon Faucher in France, with their remedies of technical education, profit-sharing and state-compensation for workers displaced by the development of machine-technology, are typical examples of this kind; they have, as the *Manifesto* says, to mitigate the harsher consequences of capitalism without interfering with the relations of production upon which it is based. The reference to free trade is, I think, pretty obviously an arrow launched against Cobden and Bright and their supporters in the Anti-Corn Law League who believed that the social problem would be solved by the adoption of universal free trade; and this view is the more likely since both Marx and Engels, and especially Engels, had seen at first hand how the propaganda of the League had done much to break the hold of the Chartist Movement upon the workers. It is reasonable to suppose that the reference to tariffs is primarily a thrust at Friedrich List—who had died only the year before—and his system of German national economy based upon a closed customs union as the unit of prosperity. If this is so, it links the *Manifesto* to the growing economic literature from America, the famous *Report on Manufacture* (1791) of Alexander Hamilton, for example, and the works of Henry C. Carey, to which we know Marx and Engels gave careful attention, though without being convinced that the protectionists had found an answer to the central issue of productive relations. What they were rejecting was the notorious doctrine of the "harmony of interest" between capital and labour, which, though Adam Smith at the rise and

John Stuart Mill at the end of the first half-century of classical political economy had already seen it to be fallacious, was still the main ground upon which the growth of trade unions was discouraged and repressed. Men of good will, the *Manifesto* says in effect, can never build a society capable of justice by philanthropy of palliatives. It is nothing less than the whole system of productive relations that must be changed.

In a sense, the final section on previous socialist literature, which deals with what the *Manifesto* calls "critico-Utopian" writers, is a little disappointing. It quite properly emphasises the fact that the literature of the first proletarian strivings produces "fantastic pictures" of future society, that it thinks of the workers as a suffering rather than a revolutionary class, that it appeals, for the most part, to ethical principles beyond and above class-antagonism, that it seeks to change society "by peaceful means" and "by small experiments." It agrees that Babeuf, Owen, Cabet and Fourier attack the existing foundation of their civilisation at its roots, that they are "full of the most valuable materials for the enlightenment of the working class." But their proposals are dismissed as "purely Utopian," and though it is admitted that they were themselves "in many respects revolutionary," it is insisted that their followers have always "formed merely reactionary sects." "They therefore endeavour," wrote Marx and Engels, "and that consistently, to deaden the class struggle, and to reconcile the class-antagonisms. . . . They sink into the category of the reactionary conservative socialists, differing from them only by more systematic pedantry." They became, we are told, the violent opponents of working-class political action. Like the followers of Owen who oppose the Chartists, and the followers of Fourier who oppose the *Reformistes*, they have a "fanatical and superstitious belief in the miraculous effects of their social science."

The praise is grudging, and a good deal of the criticism is, in fact, unfair. It is unfair to Babeuf, to whom, through Buonarrotti, the debt of Marx and Engels themselves was great. It is unfair to a great deal of Bronterre O'Brien's work, to the remarkable trade union achievements of John Doherty, and to the profound writer in the *Poor Man's Guardian* of 1831 whom Beer, the careful historian of British socialism, has given good reasons for thinking was a self-educated working man. No doubt it is fair to conclude that Owen and Saint-Simon, Hodgskin and Fourier, with all their piercing insight into social conditions, never had faith enough in the working class to believe that it could accomplish its own emancipation, or enough interest in political action to recognise the real nature and function of the state-power. But it ought to be compared with the tribute—which Marx approved—paid to Owen, Saint-Simon and Fourier by Engels in 1874 in his preface to the reprint, as a book, of the article he had written in 1850 for the *Neue Rheinische Zeitung* on the Peasants' War in Germany of the sixteenth century. "Just as German theoretical socialism will never forget," he wrote, "that it rests on [their] shoulders . . . three men who, in spite of all their fantastic notions and Utopianism, have their places among the most eminent thinkers of all times, and whose genius anticipated innumerable ideas the correctness of which we are now scientifically proving, so the practical workers' movement in Germany must never forget that it has developed on the shoulders of the English and French movements, that it was able directly to utilise their hardly-bought experience, and that it could now avoid the mistakes that were unavoidable at the time they made them. Without the English trade unions and the French workers' political struggles before them, without the great impulse given, in particular, by the Paris Commune, where should we be now?" And that eulogy was repeated in the quite masterly preface which Engels wrote to the English edition of 1892, of his *Socialism, Utopian and Scientific.* There, though the same point is made as in the *Manifesto* itself, it is made in a perspective far more just and profound. "Scientific socialism," as Engels again wrote in a footnote to a German reprint of the same work, "is not an exclusively German, but just as much an international, product."

What is the reason for this difference of emphasis? It lies, I suggest, in the desire to show in the *Manifesto* that "true" socialism is a species of the genus Utopian socialism and can make no claim to be regarded as scientific. Marx and Engels belittled the achievements of the Utopians in 1847 because their victory over men like Grün and Hess in Germany itself was not yet complete, and the valuation they then made of their great predecessors was part of a polemic in which they were not yet sure of victory. In 1878, their outlook held the field, still more fully in 1892; and they could afford to be more generous about the men who laid the foundations of the edifice they themselves had brought so remarkably to completion. That is essentially the attitude of Marx himself when he sought to assess his own personal contribution to socialist philosophy.[1]

# VI

The final section of the *Manifesto* is essentially an outline of the correct Communist strategy in view of the coming struggle. The Communists, it affirms, will fight for the immediate interests of the workers, without losing sight of the need to assist the emergence of the future in their aid to the present. Thus, if in France they support the social democrats—the party led by Ledru-Rollin—that will not prevent them from seeking to correct the tendencies in that party which are no more than an empty tradition handed down from the Revolution; if in Germany they support the bourgeoisie in its revolutionary struggle against absolute monarchy, the feudalism of the landlords and the reactionary outlook of the petty-bourgeois elements, that will not prevent them from awakening the workers to the realisation that, once the bourgeois revolution has been accomplished, the proletarian revolution must begin.

The Communists concentrate their efforts on Germany, Marx and Engels say, because a successful bourgeois revolution there, in the conditions of the

[1] *Letters to Kugelmann*, 12 April 1871.

nineteenth century, where the proletariat is so much more advanced than it could have been either at the time of the English or of the French Revolutions, is bound to be the prelude to an "immediate and subsequent" proletarian revolution. Their general position assumes three clear principles. They must support every revolutionary movement against the conditions of the time. They must make the question of property—that is, the ownership of the means of production—the central issue in every movement in which they participate. They must, finally, "labour everywhere for the union and agreement of the democratic parties of all countries." Their position is thus unmistakable. They will always support working-class parties, even when these are not communist, without forming a separate party of their own; even though such a party may have an inadequate programme, its proletarian character makes it the appropriate instrument through which to exercise communist influence. Where the party they support, like that of Ledru-Rollin, is not proletarian, they support it because it offers the workers the chance first of a greater rôle in politics, and second, of great social reforms.

The position of the *Manifesto* on Germany needs a somewhat more elaborate analysis. It says quite clearly that Germany is on the eve of a bourgeois revolution, and that its makers must be supported because their success will be the prelude to a proletarian revolution. We have to put this affirmation alongside the insistence of Marx and Engels themselves, at the Communist Congress in London, not many weeks before the writing of the *Manifesto* that the antagonism between the bourgeoisie and the workers is more developed in England—an inference clearly drawn from their judgment upon Chartism—than in any other country. We must compare it further, as Charles Andler has pointed out in his remarkable commentary on the *Manifesto*,[1] with the passage in Marx's article on the Hegelian philosophy of Law, published in 1844, where he argued that Germany could no longer make a partial revolution, since the only class in Germany capable of revolutionary action was the "class of the purely *déclassés.*" That class could not, in his submission of 1844, seek for any rights but those of all humanity, since it had been bowed down by suffering to a point where nothing less would enable it to reaffirm its manhood. It thus, in his view, became the proletariat; and when it made its revolution it would, by suppressing itself, inaugurate the classless society.

The change in the *Manifesto*, compared with the article of 1844, admits of a simple explanation. As Andler rightly points out, in the three years that intervened between them Marx himself had ceased to be a "true" socialist, like Grün and Hess, and had come to realise the full significance of historical materialism. He no longer, therefore, thought conceptually, but concretely, of the German workers; and he realised in 1847 that they could not move directly to revolutionary emancipation since German capitalism had not yet developed sufficiently to make them in a full sense a proletariat bent on freeing itself by revolution from its chains. This was later pointed out

[1] *La Manifeste Communiste, Introduction Historique et Commentaire* (Paris, 1901), p. 204.

by Engels in the remarkable articles he wrote for the New York *Tribune* in 1861–2.[1] "The working-class movement itself," he wrote, "is never independent, is never of an exclusively proletarian character, until all the different elements in the middle class and, particularly, its most progressive element, the large manufacturers, have conquered political power, and remodelled the state in terms of their needs. It is then that the inevitable conflict between the employer and the employed becomes imminent, and cannot be adjourned any longer; that the working class can no longer be put off with delusive topics, and promises never to be realised; that the great problem of the nineteenth century, the abolition of the proletariat, is at last brought forward fairly, and in its proper light."

The reason why Marx and Engels in the years immediately preceding 1848 looked to Germany for the revolution they were expecting has, I think, one personal and two historical grounds. The first is that they were, after all, Germans, with the passionate nostalgia of the exile for his native land; no one can fail to see in their correspondence that, with all the width of their interest in other countries, the interest they took in German development had an intensity which put it on a different plane. They recognised, moreover, that the revolutionary content had, at least for the time being, gone out of the English movement, as was proved in the abortive Chartist

[1] *Germany: Revolution and Counter-Revolution.* These articles, first published as a book in England in 1896, were long supposed to have been written by Marx. It is, of course, clear that Engels wrote them in the fullest consultation with him. The quotation in the text is from the first article.

demonstration in London on 10 April 1848, and that it would provide no opportunity of vital change. But in Germany, as Engels wrote in the New York *Tribune*, in the second of his articles, "people were either constitutional monarchists or more or less clearly defined socialists or communists." So sharp an antithesis made it natural, therefore, to look to Germany for some important opportunity. "With such elements," wrote Engels, "the slightest collision must have brought about a great revolution. While the higher nobility and the older civil and military officers were the only safe supporters of the existing system; while the lower nobility, the trading middle classes, the universities, the schoolmasters of every degree, and even part of the lower ranks of the bureaucracy and military officers, were all united against the government; while behind these there stood the dissatisfied masses of the peasantry, and of the proletarians of the large towns, supporting, for the time being, the Liberal Opposition, but already muttering strange words about taking things into their own hands; while the bourgeoisie was ready to hurl down the government, and the proletarians were preparing to hurl down the bourgeoisie in its turn; this government continued obstinately in a course which must bring about a coalition. Germany was, in the beginning of 1848, on the eve of a revolution; and this revolution was sure to come, even had the French Revolution of February not hastened it."

That explains the special significance the *Manifesto* attached to German events. But Marx and Engels did not look upon those events as isolated and complete in themselves. They were a part only of a much vaster perspective in which the proletariat of one country could be seen handing on the revolutionary torch to the proletariat of another. That is why the *Manifesto* appeals to the workers of all countries to unite. The famous sentence which concludes it is not the formula of an empty ritual. It is inherent in the whole *Manifesto* as an expression of the interdependence of a class which, as capitalist society takes the whole world into its grasp, must act internationally if it is to act successfully. It is the anticipation of what Marx was to say, some sixteen years later, in his inaugural address to the First International. "To conquer political power," he told the meeting in St. Martin's Hall,[1] "has become the great duty of the working classes . . . One element of success they have—numbers; but numbers weigh only in the balance if united by combination, and led by knowledge. Past experience has shown how disregard of that bond of brotherhood which ought to exist between the workmen of different countries, and incite them to stand firmly by each other in all their struggles for emancipation, will be chastised by the common discomfiture of their incoherent efforts . . . The emancipation of the working classes requires their fraternal concurrence." The men who had lived through ardour to failure in 1848 were there reaffirming their conviction that the "immediate combination of the still disconnected movements" in different countries was the indispensable condition of working-class emancipation; to achieve it was not "a local nor a national, but a social, problem, embracing all countries in which mod-

[1] *Selected Works*, vol. II, p. 440.

ern society exists, and depending for its solution on the concurrence, practical and theoretical, of the most advanced countries." So only could the workers throw off their chains.

# VII

Time has added to the lustre of the *Communist Manifesto*; and it has achieved the remarkable status not only of being a classic, but a classic also which is directly relevant to the controversies which rage a century after it was written. Inevitably, therefore, it has become the subject of rival interpretations; and it is not seldom read as though its eminent authors were still fighting for one or another of the different schools of contemporary socialist thought. It is, indeed, hardly an exaggeration to say that, under the leadership of the Communist Party of Soviet Russia, an attempt has been made to secure the prestige of the *Manifesto* for those only who accept the leadership and direction of Moscow, and to argue that it has no meaning outside the canons of orthodoxy which first Lenin, and later Stalin, have applied to its scrutiny. One may go even further and suggest that those who do not accept these canons are regarded by the adherents of the Muscovite school with the same furious indignation as Marx and Engels regarded the "true" socialists of their own day.

Of certain things there can be no doubt at all.

*Harold J. Laski*

Marx and Engels were both convinced that the victory of the proletariat, and the consequential establishment of a classless society would normally be established by violent revolution. They were convinced, also, that only by the alliance of the working classes in the most advanced countries would a proletarian revolution in any one of them be able to hope that its successful consolidation might be seriously expected. They were emphatic that Communists must not form a party which separates itself from the mass organisations of the working class; and they insisted that Communists must, while they ceaselessly bear in view the ultimate and decisive proletarian revolution, never forget the high importance of helping to realise those lesser, if more immediately realisable, gains which improve the position of the worker. They were ready to make alliances with non-working-class parties, if the result of their joint action was strategically progressive. When, jointly, they re-published the *Manifesto* in 1872, they remarked that while its "general principles . . . are, on the whole, as correct to-day as ever," nevertheless "the practical application of the principles will depend, as the *Manifesto* itself states, everywhere and at all times, on the historical conditions for the time being existing." On that account, they said, the revolutionary measures they proposed in 1848 needed "no special stress." They thought, also, that the immense industrial development since the *Manifesto* first appeared, as well as "the practical experience" of the February Revolution and of the Commune made some of the measures obsolete. Above all, they argued, one thing especially was proved by the Commune, viz., that "the working

61

class cannot simply lay hold of the ready-made state machinery, and wield it for its own purposes." This last sentence is a quotation from Marx's famous pamphlet, the *Civil War in France*; and in a letter written to Kugelmann on 12 April 1871,[1] during the existence of the Paris Commune, Marx explained what this meant by referring his German admirer to the last chapter of his *Eighteenth Brumaire* where "you will find that I say that the next attempt of the French Revolution will be no longer, as before, to transfer the bureaucratic-military machine from one hand to the other, but to *smash* it; and this is essential for every real people's revolution on the Continent." The virtue of the Commune was that it was elected by universal suffrage, had a majority of working men "or acknowledged representatives of the working class," and was "a working, not a parliamentary body, executive and legislative at the same time," the members being elected for short terms, and subject to recall. In his preface to the reprint in 1891 of the *Civil War in France*, Engels wrote that "of late, the Social Democratic Philistine has once more been filled with wholesome terror at the words 'Dictatorship of the Proletariat.' Well and good, gentlemen, do you want to know what the Dictatorship looks like? Look at the Paris Commune. That was the Dictatorship of the Proletariat."

Almost all these phrases have been the subject of violent conflict, of which the best known, perhaps, is that between Lenin and Trotsky, in one camp, and the German social democrat Karl Kautsky in the

---

[1] Cf. Lenin's comment, preface to *Letters to Kugelmann* (London, 1934), pp. 16–19.

other; Rosa Luxembourg, who was martyred in the Spartacus revolt of 1919, and the Russian Menshevik leader, Jules Martov, may fairly be described as occupying an intermediate position between the two extreme interpretations. It is impossible here to enter upon the kind of detailed and special scrutiny of texts in which not only is every word important, but in which, also, what is really a subjective valuation of their importance in their total context, plays a very considerable part. It must suffice to examine certain major themes in the dispute, and, somewhat dogmatically, to suggest the main results of research about them.

It is quite clear that both Marx and Engels expected that most proletarian revolutions would be successful only after heavy fighting, and that the only possible exceptions they saw to this rule were Great Britain, the United States and, perhaps, Holland. They thought that the critical moment would come for Great Britain when Ireland and India had secured their independence, since this would deprive Great Britain of a source of exploitation which enabled it, in a considerable degree, to give its proletariat a bourgeois character and outlook. They were confident that, in all cases, the arrival of the working class in power would mean a period of transition marked by the dictatorship of the proletariat.

No phrase has been subject to so much misinterpretation as the "dictatorship of the proletariat." Let us be clear at once that neither for Marx nor for Engels was it the antithesis of democracy; for them, its antithesis was the "dictatorship of the bourgoisie" which, as they believed, obtained in every country, even when concealed by formally democratic politi-

soft view of Mx-Eng

cal institutions, so long as the ownership of the means of production remained in middle-class hands. Marx and Engels meant by the "dictatorship of the proletariat" an organisation of society in which the state-power was in the hand of the working class, and used with all the force necessary to prevent it being seized from them by the class which formerly exercised its authority. They assume that the representatives of the working class will use the state-power to change the relations of production and to repress any attempt to interfere with this change. But it is obvious from Engels' identification of the Paris Commune with proletarian dictatorship that he regards it as based on the support of the majority, that it employs the technique of universal suffrage, and that its acceptance of the people's rights to frequent elections, and to the recall of their representatives implies full popular participation in the working of the dictatorship. It is obvious, further, from Marx's account of the Commune as a legislature and executive in one, that it denies the validity of the separation of powers, and assumes that the dictatorship is exercised through the elected body based upon popular choice and subject to public opinion, through the right of each constituency to recall any representative it may have chosen; that, surely, was what Marx meant when he wrote that "nothing could be more foreign to the spirit of the Commune than to supersede universal suffrage by hierarchic investiture." Marx even points out that the "great bulk of the Paris middle class . . . the wealthy capitalist alone excepted" admitted that "this was the first revolution in which the working class was openly acknowledged as the only class capable of social initiative;" he noted that it supplied the republic with the basis of really democratic institutions; and he compares the peace and order it secured within Paris, with the fanatically repressive atmosphere of Versailles under the domination of Thiers.

From this angle, it seems to me inescapable that Marx and Engels did not conceive the dictatorship of the proletariat to mean the dictatorship of the Communist Party over the rest of the community, that is, the centralisation of the state-power in the hands of a single party, which imposes its will by force on all citizens outside its ranks. It is conceivable that the struggle for the state-power may be so intense that the government has no alternative but to proclaim a state of siege until it has consolidated its authority. It is undeniable, also, that a workers' government in possession of the state-power may find it necessary to penalise persons or parties who threaten its safety, in the same way as the British Government found it necessary to assume drastic powers when it was threatened by invasion after Dunkirk in 1940. It was, I think, this second situation that Marx and Engels had in view. They assumed that the use of the state-power by and for the workers would mean an expansion, and not a contraction, of democratic forces; it would permit, that is, vastly greater numbers to participate in social life effectively than is possible when democratic institutions operate only within the framework of capitalist production. They could not, therefore, have envisaged the Communist Party acting as a dictatorship over the working class and excluding all other parties from the right to share in, and influence over, the exercise of power.

I think this view is borne out by other evidence. The *Maniefsto* itself declares quite explicitly that Communists are the vanguard of the working class. They are not its masters; they are in the forefront of the co-operative effort to abolish capitalist society. Still more important, the Communists do not form a separate party of their own. They ally themselves with other organisations, especially of the working class, which aim at the same end as themselves, or may objectively be regarded as assisting that end even though unconsciously. That was why, for example, the Communist League supported Ledru-Rollin in 1845, even though he hated Communism. That was why, also, they persuaded the First International to support the Paris Commune, and why those of its members, who were also members of the International, cooperated in its heroic struggle with others who did not belong to it. Unless, indeed, Marx and Engels had taken this view, they would have been arguing that the dictatorship of the proletariat means the rule of that party leadership to the guidance of which any political organisation of large size must give heavy responsibilities. They never argued for this outlook. On the contrary, their deepest concern was to make the state-power, when it passed into the workers' hands, not only the organ through which the capitalist relations of production were transformed into socialist relations of production, but the organ also through which the unreal democracy of capitalist society became the real democracy of socialist society. Repression in all its forms was for them a transitory necessity. That was why they

66

could argue that, with the establishment of socialism, the state would "wither away."

The "withering away" of the state is another famous phrase that has been much discussed and much misunderstood. In one sense it is a purely logical inference from the definition of the *Manifesto*. The state is there defined as the "executive committee of the bourgeoisie." Obviously, therefore, as the power to govern is taken out of the hands of the bourgeoisie by the workers, the state as a bourgeois institution ceases to exist because being in the workers' hands it becomes transformed into a proletarian institution. Marx and Engels then argued that its coercive authority, the army, for example, the police, and the civil service, would have so to be adapted as to be capable of use by the workers for socialist purposes, as they had been adapted by the bourgeoisie to be used for capitalist purposes. They thought in 1872, as Marx had suggested 20 years before, that a socialist society would have to "break" the political machinery of the régime it took over in order to make the adaptation successful. What did they mean by "breaking" the machinery of the capitalist state? The answer is, I think, that it was to be deprived of that character of an "hierarchical investiture" which, as Marx had written in *Civil War in France*, prevented the defective power of numbers from being authoritative. The organs of government were to be genuinely democratised. They were to be in and of the new proletarian society, not, as in capitalist society, over and above the workers, separated from them by caste-like walls, so that they could impose upon the workers the discipline necessary to maintain in its fullness the capitalist mode of production. The defence forces, the police and the civil service were to have no special privileges, and no special place in the new régime. Their members were to be looked upon as workers performing a necessary social function in the same way as any other groups of workers. They were to be deprived of their "hierarchical" attributes.

It should be added that when Marx and Engels spoke of the "withering away of the state" there is no reason to suppose they believed that in a socialist country the hopes of the philosophical anarchists would be fulfilled and that all authority would be the outcome of express assent to its orders. No doubt both of them strongly believed that as the private ownership of the means of production passed away there would be far less need for a coercive apparatus in society. That was a natural view for them to take since they held that it was the private ownership of those means which was responsible for most of what was evil in the social process. Their insistence that the state-power was essentially used to protect that private ownership from attack was, of course, held with great emphasis by Adam smith himself. "It is only under the shelter of the civil magistrates," Adam Smith wrote,[1] "that the owner of that valuable property, acquired by the labour of many years, or perhaps many successive generations, can sleep a single night in security." Marx and Engels agreed with the implications in Adam Smith's statement, though the inference they would have drawn was different. But there is nothing to suggest in all they wrote that with the establishment of a socialist soci-

[1] *Wealth of Nations.* Bk. V, chap. 1, S. 2.

ety government itself becomes unnecessary. They rarely spoke of what a socialist society would be like; and the few references they did make to its character only justify us in saying that they looked to a fuller and freer expression of individuality when the capitalists' fetters upon the forces of production had been finally removed.

Some discussion is desirable of the materialist conception of history which is the vital thread upon which the whole of the *Communist Manifesto* hangs; the more so because it continues to be strangely misrepresented by historians and social philosophers. It is not a claim that all actions are the result of economic motives. It does not insist either that all change is economically caused. It does not mean that the ideas and behaviour of men are fatalistically predetermined and that, whether he will or no, the emergence of a socialist society is inevitable. It is the argument that, as Engels puts it,[1] "production and, with production, the exchange of its products, is the basis of every social order; that in every society which has appeared in history, the distribution of the products, and, with it, the division of society into classes or estates, is determined by what is produced, and how it is produced, and how the product is exchanged." This is the basis from which Marx and Engels were led to that philosophy of history which led them to part company with their former allies, the Left Hegelians, whose conceptions are attacked in the *Manifesto*. For it led them to see that the way in which the total social production is divided in a community is not the outcome of the pur-

[1] *Socialism, Utopian and Scientific*, S. 3.

poses, either good or bad, of the members of the community, but of the legal relations which arise out of given modes of production, and that these legal relations are independent of the wills of those engaged in production. Since changes in the modes of production and exchange are ceaselessly taking place, legal relations which were, at one time, adapted to the conditions of that time, cease to be adapted to them. It is in this disproportion between legal relations in the community and the forces of production in it that the changes in men's ideas of good and bad, justice and injustice, are to be found. That class in a community which legally owns the means of production uses the state-power to sanction that division of the product of which it approves. It therefore seeks through the coercive authority at the disposal of the state-power, to compel the general acceptance of its approved division; and systems of values, political, ethical, religious, philosophical, are ways in which, directly or indirectly, men express their agreement or disagreement with the nature of the division which the owners of the instruments of production endeavour to impose.

This does not mean that changes may be regarded as irrelevant to the ideas of men; but it does mean that men's ideas are continually evolving as their minds come to realise that changes in the methods of production and exchange render some ideas obsolete and require new ideas. As feudalism became transformed into capitalism, the legal relations it implied hindered the full use of the forces of production. The values the feudal system had been able to maintain before the advent of the capitalist method of production emerged became no longer acceptable. Then, as Engels wrote, "the bourgeoisie shattered the feudal system, and, on its ruins established the bourgeois social order, the realm of free competition, freedom of movement, equal rights for commodity owners and all the other bourgeois glories." Now, the *Manifesto* argues, changes in the forces of production have rendered the legal relations of capitalism obsolete in their turn; and socialism emerges as the claim to new relations, and, therefore, to new values which the workers, as the class which suffers most from this obsolescence, seek to put in its place.

No serious observer supposes that the materialist conception of history is free from difficulties, or that it solves all the problems involved in historical interpretation. But no serious observer either can doubt that it has done more in the last hundred years to provide a major clue to the causes of social change than any other hypothesis that has been put forward. There can really be no valid reason to deny that, over the whole space of recorded history, class struggle has been a central principle of its development. Nor can it be denied that class struggle is intimately bound up with the relations of production in some given society and the ability to develop the full possibilities of the forces of production at any given time. It is equally clear, on any close analysis, that the class which owns the instruments of production uses the state-power to safeguard that ownership, and seeks to repress the emergence of ideas and values which call that ownership into question. Anyone, moreover, who examines objectively any period in which the mode of production is rapidly changing, the age of the Reformation, for example, or the period between the two world wars, cannot fail to note that they are also periods marked by the grave instability of traditional values and of traditional institutions. There is nothing in the theory of the *Manifesto* which argues more than that the occurrence of such a period means that, if the traditional values and institutions continue to function in the new economic setting, they will deprive large numbers of their means of living, and that they will, therefore, seek to emancipate themselves from a position of which they are the victims. To do so, as Marx and Engels point out, they must possess themselves of the state-power that they may adapt the relations of production to the implications of the new order. And, on the argument of the *Manifesto*, since the passage from capitalist to social ownership marks the end of a history in which the instruments of production have been predominantly the possession of one class, the transition to public ownership means, when it is successfully effected, the emergence of the classless society.

It is this doctrine which the *Manifesto* is concerned to get accepted by socialists as against the other doctrines with which it was competing. It was not enough, Marx and Engels were saying in effect, for some men or group of men to proclaim a new principle as true and hope by the force merely of rational argument to persuade others to see also that it is true. What makes the new principle acceptable is the fact that changes in the mode of production have produced the material environment which makes it seem the natural expression of what people want. The duty to be tolerant is rarely likely to receive wide acceptance when it is advanced as an abstract metaphysical obligation. But when intolerance hinders the attainment by society of a full command over its material resources, men begin to see a validity in arguments advanced on its behalf, some religious, some ethical, some political, some economic, the strength of which had not previously been apparent to them. All the world applauded Robert Owen so long as he made the operation of that "revolution" in the mind and practice of the "human race" a philanthropic experiment confined to his own factories in New Lanark. But when he argued that his principles were so obviously rational that all social organisation should be adapted to their application, the world turned angrily upon him and showed him that, in the absence of the necessary material conditions, a principle which has justice and truth and reason on its side will still be unable to conquer the world by the inherent force of its own virtue. It is not until men see that the "anarchy of social production" caused by capitalism in decay can be replaced "by a socially planned regulation of production in accordance with the needs both of society as a whole, and of each individual," that they are prepared to get rid of capitalism.

"The forces operating in society," wrote Engels,[1] "work exactly like the forces operating in nature: blindly, violently, destructively, so long as we do not understand them and fail to take them into account. But when we once have recognised them, and understood how they work, their direction and their efforts, the gradual subjection of them to our will, and the use of them for the attainment of our aims, depends entirely upon ourselves. And this is quite es-

[1] *Socialism, Utopian and Scientific,* S. 3.

pecially true of the mighty, productive forces of the present day." That is, I think, the central principle which underlies the whole of the *Communist Manifesto;* it is the social application of Bacon's great aphorism that "nature, to be commanded, must be obeyed." It is our attempt to show that every pattern of social institutions presupposes a stage in the development of productive forces, and that those who seek for the achievement of the pattern in which they believe will succeed only if their aim is justified by the character of those productive forces at the time when they make their effort. That was why, though Carlyle and Ruskin saw the evils of their own day, their remedy was an anachronism when they preached it; they preached a sermon to men who, as it were, had already left their church. That was why, to take a contemporary instance, the New Deal of President Roosevelt was able only to assuage temporarily the wounds he sought to heal; for those wounds were not some temporary infliction, but the symptoms of a disease far more deep and deadly than he was prepared to recognise.

One last aspect of the *Manifesto* required to be clarified. Why was it given this title? Those who sponsored it had not thought of it in that form; it was rather a catechism, more easily capable of being memorised, that they had in mind. The word "Communism" had no special sanctity for them; their organisation, in one or another of its forms, had operated under a variety of names. It is not a question we can answer with any certainty; Engels himself did not deal with it in the recollections he wrote later—themselves not always accurate—of how it came to be composed in the form in which we have it. Perhaps it was a "Manifesto" in half-conscious tribute to the memory of the Babouvian *Manifeste des Egaux*,[1] a salute to one of the supreme documents of that French Revolution which Marx and Engels recognised as one of the great climacterics of history, and from which they learned so much; perhaps it is also due to a faint recollection of the once well-known pamphlet which Victor Considerant had published shortly before.

Why "communist" and not "socialist" Manifesto? Obviously, in the first instance, because it was the official publication of the Communist League. We have little other evidence on which to base speculations. It was possibly the outcome of a recollection of the Paris Commune in the French Revolution, an institution to which all socialists did homage. It was possibly a desire to distinguish the ideas for which they stood from socialist doctrines which they were criticising so severely. The one thing that is certain, from the document itself, is that the choice of the term "Communist" was not intended to mark any organisational separation between the Communist League and other socialist or working-class bodies. On the contrary, Marx and Engels were emphatic in their insistence that the Communists do not form a separate Party and that they ally themselves with all the forces which work towards a socialist society. The idea of a separate communist party dates from the Russian Revolution; it had no place in the thought either of Marx or of Engels.

---

[1] Written by Sylvan Maréchal.

# VIII

Those who formulate a new social philosophy rarely remain the masters of its fate. Once it has begun to exercise a serious influence it acquires a prestige value as a weapon which makes its later adherents look upon it as something to which they can give the special shape they desire for the special purposes they have in view. At that stage it is always in danger of becoming an orthodox dogma, any development of which is regarded as a heresy unless it becomes directly associated with some outstanding success in action. No better example of this exists perhaps, then the social philosophy enunciated by St. Paul in his *Epistle to the Romans* for the nascent Christian Churches. It is a body of doctrine difficult to reconcile with what we can gather of the teaching of Jesus Christ which has, in fact, little interest in social philosophy and has its centre of interest outside a world to the imminent end of which it looks forward. But St. Paul, who was a great statesman as well as a great theologian, was concerned to safeguard the future of his fellow-believers; and he set out for them a code of political behaviour which would minimise the danger of any conflict between the petty churches of his day and the mighty Roman empire, at least for the period in which the clamant hostility of those churches to Rome might well have jeopardised their survival. It is not until, under Constantine, they were accepted as the official religion, and the meek begin to inherit the earth, that new and bolder implications are found in the Pauline doctrine. It would be interesting to know what one who originally accepted the precepts of the *Epistle to the Romans* would have thought of St. Ambrose's thunderous denunciation of Theodosius.

Anyone who considers the subsequent history of the *Communist Manifesto,* especially after Engels' death, will recongise how, in much the same way as under the Pauline doctrine, warring sects among the socialists it helped so much to create took charge of its destiny. Neither Marx nor Engels, of course, ever surrendered their belief that violent revolution would accompany the victory of socialism in most national communities. But, after Bismarck repealed the anti-socialist laws in Germany and the Social Democratic Party there began, despite all opposition, to make both constant and remarkable gains, Engels began to set the art of revolution in an importantly different perspective. Nowhere is this seen so clearly as in the perface he wrote, dated 8 March 1895, to a new reprint of Marx's *Class Struggles in France.* That new perspective, it may be suggested, is marked by four major principles. The first is the recognition that universal suffrage was not merely, as the disillusion after the failures of 1848 had persuaded so many workers, especially in the Latin countries, a deception; it becomes also a weapon of emancipation. "With this successful utilisation of universal suffrage," he wrote, "an entirely new mode of proletarian struggle came into force, and this quickly developed further . . . the bourgeoisie and the government came to be much more afraid of the legal than of the illegal action of the Workers' Party, of the results of elections than of those of rebellion." "The irony of world history," he remarked in a later passage, "turns everything upside-down. We, the 'Revolutionaries,' the 'Rebels,' we are thriving far better on legal methods, than on illegal methods and revolts. The parties of order, as they call themselves, are perishing under the legal conditions created by themselves. They are despairingly with Odillon-Barrot: *la légalité nous tue,* legality is the death of us; whereas we, under this legality, get firm muscles, and rosy cheeks, and look like eternal life; and if we are not so crazy as to let ourselves be driven into street fighting, in order to please them, then nothing else is finally left to them but themselves to break through this legality so faithful to them."

This, then, is the first principle set out by Engels. Universal suffrage may be so successful an instrument of socialist progress that it only pays anti-socialist governments where recourse is had by socialists to rebellion; indeed, anti-socialist governments themselves may be driven into illegal action for fear of the results of constitutionalism. From this first principle, there follows a second which is mainly the result of technological change. "All the conditions on the insurgents' side have grown worse," he wrote. "An insurrection with which all sections of the people sympathise will hardly recur . . . The 'people,' therefore, will always appear divided, and, with this, a powerful lever, so extraordinarily effective in 1848, is lacking." The new weapons, and the new technical organisation, not least the actual character of the organisation of

towns, all make the barricades practically useless.
The time for the extempore revolution is over. There
may be street fighting in the future. But it can only
be successful when "the masses themselves have already grasped what is at stake, what they are going
in for, body and soul. But in order that the masses
may understand what is to be done, long, persistent
work is required."

The third principle upon which Engels insists is
that, properly organised, the growth of socialist
strength among the masses drives the reactionary
forces to unconstitutional action. That growth can
only be checked "by revolt on the part of the parties
of order, which cannot live without breaking the
laws." The threat to order thus comes from the
Right. It is then in the difficulty that, like the socialists before 1848, the Right can only break the Constitution so long as it has the government, and,
therefore, the state-power, the army, above all, in its
hands. And Engels draws attention to the early history of Christianity to suggest that, once a great
idea has permeated the masses, it will undermine
the foundations of the state, will infect the army,
and will only be impeded by persecution from
reaching its goal.

The fourth principle follows from this. Revolutions
are not won "by one mighty stroke," nor can "the
revolution of the minority be turned into the revolution of the majority," without an intellectual maturity on the part of the masses; this itself is the
proportionate outcome of economic conditions
which are ripe for revolutionary transformation because they no longer permit expansion. This intellectual maturity is no longer a sudden achievement. "It

has slowly to press forward," Engels wrote, "from position to position in a hard, tenacious struggle." Obviously when Engels wrote in this fashion he was seeking once and for all to rid socialism of its Blanquist elements, the tradition of conspiracy, the secret societies, the belief in a successful *coup d'état* effected by a revolutionary minority. He was warning the movement against the facile optimism of 1848 and its aftermath, the need to look forward "to a long struggle between the antagonistic elements concealed within the 'people' itself." Only a "world crisis" makes possible a revolutionary opportunity; and it can be used successfully only if the masses are, with full and conscious understanding, behind the purposes of the revolution it is sought to achieve.

When Lenin wrote his famous <u>State and Revolution</u> in 1917 he built the main structure of its arguments on the lessons drawn by Marx and Engels over the generation following its failure. But it is important to realise that the term he gave to Marxist doctrine had already received a special colour from Russian conditions, and that much of his own outlook was the result of his own struggle, first, to get a majority in the Russian Social Democratic Party, and then to maintain that majority, both before and after the abortive revolution of 1905, in extraordinarily difficult conditions. He won the majority at the Conference of 1903. What, however, he won it for was a set of organisational and strategic ideas which were largely unconnected with philosophic speculation. That is clear from the fact that, by 1904, when Lenin had lost the support of Plekhanov, and his control over *Iskra* and the central Committee of the party, he gladly accepted the support of Bogdanov and his friends. That he disagreed with the main philosophic idea of Bogdanov we know from his correspondence; Plekhanov, indeed, sneered at him for doing so, and told him that just as Leninist strategy was a revision of Marxist strategy, so the philosophy of Bogdanov was a revision of Marxist philosophy. Bogdanov was an idealist of the Kantian school deeply interested in the turn that Mach was giving to metaphysical speculation. Very significantly, Lenin, until 1908, did not think these philosophic differences important. So far as he was concerned, Bogdanov's interest in Mach and Avenarius was unimportant. "It is wholly incomprehensible to me," he said at the Third Bolshevik Conference of 1905, "what these men, for whom I haven't the slightest sympathy, have to do with the social revolution. They write on individual and social experience, or something of the sort, but really they have no ideas on the democratic dictatorship."

What is significant in this is that, from 1904 to 1907, though Lenin disagreed with the metaphysics of Bogdanov, he was untroubled by it because they agreed on revolutionary strategy. When over the elections to the Third Duma they disagreed on revolutionary strategy Lenin set out with all his relentless determination to attack Bogdanov and all his supporters. It is interesting that, while he was writing his *Materialism and Empirio-Criticism*, he was, at the same time, assuring Maxim Gorki, who was then much influenced both by Bogdanov and the "fideism" of Lunacharski, of his "most unerring judgment in artistic creation, and that, when you create such views, both out of your artistic experience and out of philosophy, even if this philosophy

81

is an idealistic one, you may come to conclusions
which may be of enormous value to the workers'
party." Yet that did not prevent him in July 1909
from using the editorial conference of *Proletarie,*
without any notice given, to expel Bogdanov and his
supporters from the Bolshevik "faction," and to out-
law their doctrines. This action, of course, overruled,
quite unconstitutionally, the decisions taken by the
London Congress of 1907 and set aside the Bolshevik centre which had been elected there. It was
expulsion, Lenin explained, from the faction and not
from the Social Democratic Party. "A party," he told
the editorial conference, "can include a wide range
of opinions, the extremes of which may even be dia-
metrically opposed to each other." But, within three
years, Lenin was arguing that only the Bolsheviks of
his own faction represented the needs of a Marxist
party, and the October Revolution made Lenin's
Bolshevik group the owners of the state-power. No
official blessing was then given to the wide and flexible outlook upon the Workers' Party of which Lenin
had written to Gorki, and of which he had spoken in
the editorial conference; then, clearly, he had regarded his own Bolshevik faction not as a separate
party, but as, in the sense of the *Communist
Manifesto,* essentially the vanguard of the party and
intimately linked to it. The virtual canonisation of
*Materialism and Empirio-Criticism,* in subsequent
years, made every branch of thought one in which
an official state-orthodoxy could be imposed with the
authority of Lenin; and denial of that orthodoxy
would enable the man guilty of deviation not merely
to be an intellectual heretic, but almost everything
else from hypocrite to a traitor to the revolutionary

82

cause. No one, I think, can understand the vitriolic character of communist polemic since 1917 who does not realise that its effective origin is a book written by Lenin less because of any sense that metaphysical differences were necessarily differences on the plane of party-action, but because, when he wrote it, he was at all costs concerned to defeat and to discredit Bogdanov lest his own views of party strategy ceased to dominate the Bolshevik faction.

I have set out this history because it illustrates so remarkably what happens when the large and flexible outlook of the *Communist Manifesto* is applied in a narrow and dogmatically rigid way. Lenin's application of Marxism to Russia has naturally had immense influence because it was the instrument of success in the October Revolution. But that influence has also had its evil and dangerous side because it has led Communists, both inside and outside Russia, to insist that the whole Leninist interpretation of Marxism, metaphysical, ethical, logical, scientific, psychological, political, economic and strategic, is the only possible way of understanding the world, and that no one outside the Communist Party can really understand either science or society. Granted the way in which the Communist Party of Soviet Russia is organised, this has come to mean that the Central Executive Committee of the Russian Communist Party—the Politbureau—is, in fact, the guardian of universal truth. Anyone accordingly who dissents from its views is rejecting universal truth and is an enemy of the only socialism that matters, which is itself, of course, that of the Russian Communist Party. This would mean that outside the Communist Party, no one can claim

to be a socialist unless he accepts the line which, at
any given time, the leaders of the Russian Communist Party announce as the correct one to be followed.

This has had certain results, the tragic character
of which it is difficult to overestimate. For since the
leaders of Russian Communism have naturally been
above all concerned to safeguard the October Revolution and to consolidate its results, their directions
to other parties, both during the lifetime of the
Third International and since its dissolution, have
been set in those terms. This has led Communists
outside Russia to follow in a docile way the directions of Moscow without any attempt at the independent assessment of their value and validity,
when they are applied to concrete situations outside
Russia, where neither the historic conditions inher-
ited there nor the actual situations confronted, make
the policy recommended by Russia either practical
or desirable.

Lenin himself had as early as 1921 to warn
Communist parties outside Russia against what he
called "the infantile malady of Left Wing Communism"—a malady which, in its essence, consisted of
an effort on the part of nascent Communist parties to
repeat in their birth-pangs all the mistakes against
which he himself had been fighting for almost a generation before 1917. But the more unhappy results
were deeper. The working-class movement was divided in most of the major countries between Communists and Social Democrats. Their hatred for one
another became far more important to each than
their antagonism to the common capitalist enemy.
Communists formed separate political parties, even

### Harold J. Laski

separate trade unions. They became so insistent that social democracy was a method of safeguarding capitalism against the workers that there was a period when they followed Moscow in proclaiming that social democrats were, in fact, social fascists. Almost down to the very advent of Hitler to power, they were ready to believe that his government was the necessary prelude to victory; they would be the residuary legatees of his inevitably rapid overthrow. When the grave error of this policy was perceived, they at once became the ardent advocates of the united front and saw no reason in the world why men whom the day before, as it were, they had been denouncing as "lacqueys of capitalism," or "betrayers of the working class," should not at once agree to admit them to the ranks of a party they had consistently announced they intended to destroy. When the "United Front" did not succeed, and Hitler, who seemed to have considerable support among capitalists in all countries, grew ever more dangerous, above all as a crusader against Soviet Russia, they accepted from Moscow the idea of the "Popular Front," in which Communists would join with any party, no matter what its outlook, so long as it was hostile to Fascism in all its forms. When, roughly by the time of Munich, it was clear that the main capitalist powers had no objection to the expansion of Hitler and Mussolini, provided that their own "vital interests" were not touched—interests which they did not regard as including the integrity of Soviet Russia—the rulers of Russia, without knowledge of Communist parties abroad, proceeded to make a treaty of friendship with Hitlerite Germany which was actually signed by Ribbentrop in Moscow one week before the outbreak of the second World War.

What is nothing less than fantastic is the intellectual gyrations performed by Communist parties in Western Europe in the period between the beginning of hostilities on 1 September 1939, and the German attack on Soviet Russia on 22 June 1941. They had been so long instructed that Hitler was the enemy of the working class everywhere, the supreme expression of capitalist reaction, that, for the first month of the war, they drew the natural inference that, as the vanguard of the working-class forces, they must take the lead in crusading for his overthrow. Their leaders, therefore, urged on the Communist rank and file the folly, as one of them put it, of merely "mouthing revolutionary phrases"; the urgent thing was to fight with all their strength against the "noxious beast." But they had forgotten the Russo-German pact, and the anxiety of Soviet leaders not to be involved in what would certainly be a destructive, and might possibly be a fatal conflict. From 7 October 1939, therefore, their whole policy changed. What had been preached as an anti-fascist crusade became a typical "imperialist" war such as was characteristic of capitalist states. It must be ended as soon as possible; there was every reason to come to terms with Hitler. For nearly two years in Great Britain, the Communist Party conducted an anti-war agitation, which included denunciation of the Labour Party as "warmongers" for entering Mr. Churchill's cabinet, an insistence that the responsibility for the war lay on the shoulders of Great Britain which was guilty of aggression against Hitlerite Germany, the encouragement of sabotage in the armament factories, and the use of the manifold disasters suffered by Great Britain after the fall of France, to insist that the prolongation of the war would destroy the working class. Then came the German attack on Russia; and, over night, the war was transformed from an imperialist war into a crusade for freedom. There was no limit to the intensity of the national effort which the Churchill government was entitled to exact, and there could be no question of peace until Hitlerite Germany had been broken in pieces. No one has ever questioned the devotion and heroism of Communist parties everywhere, above all in the countries occupied by the Fascist enemy, once Russia had entered the war. What is startling is the contrast between this and their willingness to come to terms with Hitler before his attack on Russia. Nothing in the nature of Nazism changed between 23 August 1939 and 22 June 1941, except Hitler's decision to overrun the West before, instead of after, he overran the East. Had their peace move been sucecssful, they would have immensely strengthened his position for the next attack. But they were incapable of any independent judgment upon the problem. They acted as the Russian leaders ordered them to act, without even an attempt at making a concrete analysis of the historical situation before them. They forgot altogether the significant aphorism of the Chinese Communist leader, Mao Tse-tung; "it is no use," he said, "preaching socialism unless you have a country to practise it in."

To this there must be added the grave issues created by the ethical behaviour of Communist parties outside Russia after 1917. The passion for conspiracy, the need for deception, the ruthlessness, the centralised and autocratic commands, the contempt for fair play, the willingness to use lying and treachery to discredit an opponent or to secure some desired end, complete dishonesty in the presentation of facts, the habit of regarding temporary success as justifying any measure, the hysterical invective by which they wrought to destroy the character of anyone who disagreed with them; these, in the context of an idolisation of leaders who might, the day after, be mercilessly attacked as the incarnation of evil, have been the normal behaviour of Communists all over the world. Men of extraordinary gifts ceased to have either a mind or a character of their own; they placed these in the keeping of their particular party, which, in its turn, placed them with its own mind and conscience in the keeping of Moscow, until they became automata responsive only to the orders of their leaders and accepted those orders, especially at critical moments, with a mechanical devotion which justified every shift and turn in Communist policy as the expression of infallible insight. While they were thus acting, almost in the full light of the day, they were demanding their right to be admitted into working-class organisations to which they promised complete fidelity even while it was everywhere known that their only reason for seeking that admission was their desire either to dominate or destroy the particular organization concerned, and to make it as servilely dependent upon their leaders as they were themselves.

It would be painful, and it is probably unnecessary, to document this indictment. Some of this behaviour is explained by the fact that it was the

conduct of men only just emerging from long and
evil tyranny; some of it was due to the intensity of
the persecution to which they were subjected by
reactionary opponents, especially in South-Eastern
Europe, or, as under the White terror, in Hungary.
Nor can it be denied that part of it is due to the
grave mistakes made by Social Democratic parties;
there is little that is pardonable, for example, in
those alliances concluded by Ebert and Scheide-
mann in the first days of the Weimar Republic by
which they ultimately prepared the way for the
success of counter-revolution. Nor is it possible to
forgive the cowardly and conscious betrayal of the
British Labour Party by Ramsay McDonald and a
group of his colleagues in 1931. The point of this
indictment is that the spirit of the Communist
Movement since the Russian Revolution has been in
a grave degree a denial of the spirit of the
*Manifesto,* and of the development of that spirit in
the writings of Marx and Engels after the profound
experience of 1848.

For they were, first of all, opposed to any separate
Communist Party; they appreciated always the
heavy price of splitting the working-class movement.
They recognised the necessity of a flexible application of their basic principles; at no time did they
seek mechanically to impose a dogmatic view of
their meaning upon the other socialist parties of the
world. There is no evidence to suggest that they supposed that the passage of the state-power from a
bourgeois to a working-class party would mean the
creation of a rigid dictatorship which established a
taut orthodoxy not less upon its own members, than
upon other citizens, and regarded criticism of that

orthodoxy as the supreme treason; still less is there evidence that they would have argued either that one cannot serve the cause of socialism without being a dialectical materialist, or to argue seriously that, because members of the Communist Party are dialectical materialists, they alone can hope to understand the process of science and nature and society. Both of them were fierce controversialists, accustomed to giving and taking hard blows; but they never pretended to the kind of infallibility so absolute that it is entitled to establish what is virtually an inquisition to enforce their dogmas.

So far as socialism is concerned, the essence of the Marxist view turns upon the acceptance of two vital principles. The first is that, as Marx said, "the mode of production in material life conditions the general character of the social, political and spiritual processes of life." The second principle is that so long as the instruments of production are privately owned the class which owns them uses the state-power as a coercive weapon by which to maintain its ownership. These principles, of course, are built upon certain philosophic presuppositions of which a realistic theory of knowledge is one; for, since the historical materialist believes that modes of production give birth to social relations independent of the will or consciousness of individual men, he cannot accept any metaphysical view of the world which is based on a subjective theory of knowledge. But no one would have been more emphatic than Marx and Engels, first, that the degree to which the mode of production conditions relations outside the economic field is an empirical matter upon which there may be valid difference in judgment. Nor can one believe for a moment that either Marx or Engels would have argued that even in its widest sense their social philosophy necessitated the acceptance of, say, Einstein's view of the physical nature of the universe. Anyone who remembers Marx's devotion to Shakespeare and Balzac will realise how far he was from demanding the subjection of the artist's insight to the "line" of the party at any given moment. Indeed the letter from Lenin to Gorki, which I have quoted here, shows that he shared Marx's view, as indeed, he seems to have applied it in music also, if his attitude to Balzac may be taken as a general index to his outlook.[1]

If the Communist answers this argument by saying that just as there have been immense developments in the natural sciences since Marx and Engels wrote the *Communist Manifesto,* so, clearly, there have been great developments in the social sciences, and that their interpretation of these developments has supreme validity, one is entitled to know the rational justification for this claim. As soon as this is seriously examined, it becomes clear that it is, in its essential elements, a wider expression of the extensions of Marx's theory given to it by Lenin in his effort to apply it to the special conditions of Russia. That effort was remarkably successful, and the victory of the October Revolution gave to Leninism a prestige which, intelligibly enough, outshone that of any rival view, the more so as everywhere else the attempt at revolution failed; and the chief exponents of alternative Marxist interpretations fought vainly, over large parts of the European Continent, against

[1] Cf. F. Mehring, *Karl Marx* (New York, Humanities Press, 1956), pp. 527–9.

exactly those breaches of legality by the Right
which Engels in 1895 had predicted would be the
way in which reactionary capitalism would seek to
maintain its hold on power. It is difficult not to believe that experience; the ground for this lies in the
vital decision Lenin took when, in founding the
Third International and making admission to it, as
the famous "Twenty-One Points" put to the Independent Labour Party of Great Britain made clear,
he divided the working-class movement into two sections. These have remained in most matters, if not in
theory, at least in practice, incompatible. He thus
sought to force the pace of events in Europe in the
conviction that the time was ripe for that revolution
which was to save Russia from its enemies.

In the light of these events, it is significant to
remember that, just as Engels in 1895 was convinced that the German Socialist Movement had a
special part to play in initiating the Revolution, so,
more than a generation before, Alexander Herzen, in
that exile during which his heart was always in his
own country, believed that Russia had a special destiny in the Revolution. At first he had thought that
America had a mission of the same kind, though this
faded away rapidly. What became clear to him was
an inability to "believe that the destinies of humanity and its future are fixed and nailed in Western
Europe. If Europe does not succeed in recovering
herself by a social transformation, other countries
will transform themselves." His mind turned to Russia, "full of vigour, and also full of barbarism." Social Revolution might be an idea born of Western
European experience, but he thought that it might
be adapted. "I think," he wrote, in a remarkable pas-

sage, "that there is a certain basis of truth in the fear which the Russian government is beginning to have of communism: for communism is Russian autocracy turned upside down."

Anyone who examines the writings of Marx and Engels from the moment that they moved from an acceptance of "true socialism" to their realisation of what historical materialism implied?will recognise that they contain the framework of a method which, by its very nature, excludes certain conceptions from both the theory and the practice of Marxism. It excludes the idea of a revolution made in the fashion of Blanqui; that was insisted upon by Lenin himself. It excluded also that idea of a "spontaneous" rising of the masses, which the class-conscious socialist party was then to lead to final victory, which Rosa Luxembourg advocated so ardently. For the inevitable result of any revolution so made would be the necessity of centralising power in the hands of the experienced élite, and this would obviously lead to the domination of the immature masses by that élite on the morrow of the seizure of power. That was why Engels insisted that "the great thing is to get the working class to move as a class," and argued that German Socialists in the United States committed "a grievous error" when they tried to impose their own dogmas upon the American movement. That was in 1886; and only a year later he was pointing out that the very breadth Marx gave to the general rules of the First International was the reason of its influence. "I think that all our practice has shown," he then wrote, "that it is possible to work along with the general movement of the working class at every one of its stages, without giving up or hiding our

own distinct position, and even organisation, and I
am afraid that if the German-Americans choose a
different line, they will commit a great mistake."

Lenin confronted a quite special situation. Russia
had a very small bourgeoisie, an urban working class
immensely weaker than its massive peasantry, a long
tradition, also, of evil tyranny and of popular igno-
rance. None of those conditions was present in the
Western democracies. If, after the Bolsheviks had
seized power, they had sought to govern by democratic methods, even after they had repelled foreign intervention, and repressed civil war, their
attempt to build up socialism in a single country
would have been overwhelmed by peasant opposition mainly concerned with individual possession of
the land. It was only by giving to the state-power
the character of a dictatorship in the sense defined
by Herzen, when he described communism as "Tsar-
ism turned upside down," that they were able to impose socialism on Russia. For the dictatorship
enabled them to force their country, though at an
immense price, to the verge of that industrial
maturity without which socialism is impossible.
Organisationally, it was one of the most outstanding
feats of history. But only the fanatic can deny—that
Lenin himself said[1]—that it was bound to result in
the "bureaucratic deformation" of the state-power. It
seems to me dishonest, indeed, to deny that Russian
political institutions may be regarded as maintaining
the possibility of democratisation, but, unless words
cease to have any real meaning, democratisation has
not yet seriously begun.

[1] Cf. Lenin, *Selected Works* (London, 1937), vol. IX, pp. 451f.

The revolution of which Lenin was the supreme architect was made by methods evolved by him, no doubt upon a Marxist foundation, to fit the special conditions of Russia. Its central principle adapted Marxism to those conditions by making the dictatorship of the proletariat more akin to the Jacobin idea of a Committee of Public Safety than to any content either Marx or Engels gave to that term. When they spoke of "smashing the machinery of the state," they did not mean that a state of siege must take its place; they meant that victorious socialists must cut out those features of bourgeois democracy which were incompatible with socialist democracy—the army as a special caste, for example, a bureaucracy and a judiciary hostile both by tradition and class-composition to the fulfilment of socialist purposes. This was clearly seen, as early as September, 1918, by Rosa Luxembourg. "Without general elections," she wrote,[1] "freedom of the press, freedom of the assembly, and freedom of speech, life in every public institution slows down, and becomes a caricature of itself, and bureaucracy emerges as the one deciding factor . . . Public life gradually dies, and a few score party leaders, with inexhaustible energy and limitless idealism, direct and rule. Amongst them the leadership is, in reality, in the hands of a dozen men of first-class brains, even though, from time to time an *élite* of the working class is called together in Congress to applaud the speeches of their leaders, and to vote unanimously for the resolutions they put forward."

That is a prophetic description of the relationships

[1] *Die russische Revolution* (1918), p. 113.

which emerged between the party and the working class when Lenin's theory of proletarian dictatorship was applied to Soviet Russia. Whatever may have been either its validity or its necessity in Russian conditions, or even under conditions which approximated to those of Russia, it was void of the substance of proletarian dictatorship as Marx and Engels conceived it. And when Lenin's theory has been applied on the international plane, its outcome has invariably been passionate internecine conflict, with a struggle for power in each national party; this has led to splits and schisms, with the same type of angry accusations of betrayal and immoral behaviour which Lenin, with tragic results, brought against the leaders of the Second International after the outbreak of the first World War in 1914. To think in these terms is not to think in Marxian terms. "When you enquire into the causes of the counter-revolutionary successes," wrote Engels, with the approval of Marx,[1] "there you are met on every hand with the ready reply that it was Mr. This, or Citizen That, who 'betrayed' the people. Which reply may be very true or not, according to circumstances; but under no circumstances does it explain anything, or even show how it came to pass that the 'people' allowed themselves to be thus betrayed. And what a poor chance a political party stands whose entire stock-in-trade consists in a knowledge of the solitary fact that Citizen So-and-So is not to be trusted."

This attitude, in fact, denies the whole essence of the idea for which the *Communist Manifesto* stands. The *Manifesto* did not propose the exchange of one

[1] *Revolution and Counter-Revolution* (Eng. trans. London, 1896).

dictatorship for another; it proposed the democratisation of power by putting the authority of the state into the hands of the working class. It assumes that the decline of capitalism has produced a working class mature enough to recognise that it must take its destiny into its own hands and begin the building of socialism. It does not believe that this effort can be successfully made until all the economic conditions of a particular capitalist society are ripe for it; over and over again Marx and Engels made it clear that they regarded any other view as irresponsible. Neither of them had any faith in Blanquist methods. Neither of them believed, for one moment, that, in the absence of the necessary economic conditions, some modern Committee of Public Safety, on the Jacobin model, could prematurely establish socialist relations of production by terror. Neither of them thought that the deliberate decomposition of democratic institutions would hasten the coming of socialism; on the contrary, as Engels so repeatedly said, their view was the very different one that the greater the progress of democratic institutions in a society, the more likely it was that the Right would turn from them to an eagerness for dictatorship. They regarded the destruction of democratic institutions as the supreme method a decaying capitalist reaction would employ in order to arrest the growth of that democratic class-consciousness in the workers which is the proof that the time is becoming ripe for the transition to socialism. That is why, in the famous preface to the *Critique of Political Economy*, Marx could insist that "no social order ever disappears before all the productive forces for which there is room in it, have developed; and new higher relations of production never appear before the material conditions of their existence have been matured in the womb of the old society."[1] Nothing shows more clearly that this maturity is real than the degree to which democratic institutions can withstand the effort of reaction to destroy their power to release the "new and higher relations of production" of which Marx here is speaking.

No criticism of the Leninist interpretation of the *Manifesto* means for one moment that any democratic socialist believes that there is some royal highroad down which one may pass peacefully from capitalism to socialism. The words of Marx on the trial of the Communists at Cologne are a sufficient warning on this point. "You will have to pass," he said in 1850,[2] "through fifteen, twenty, perhaps fifty years, of civil and international wars not merely in order to change conditions, but to change yourselves, and make yourselves fit to take over political power." But he did not speak in this way out of a conviction that any revolution, any *coup d'état* was itself a way by which the workers could change themselves and make themselves fit to take over political power. There are few more arresting moments in the political career of Marx and Engels than the furious attack, so dramatically described by Annenkov, on Welhelm Weitling, for his irresponsible advocacy of revolution under conditions which were unripe for its success—"The essence of his sarcastic reply," wrote Annenkov, "was that it was deception pure and simple to make the people rise

[1] *Selected Works*, vol. I, p. 356.
[2] Cf. the illuminating comment of E. H. Carr, *Karl Marx* (London, 1934), p. 104.

without showing it how solid was the basis of its action. To arouse fantastic hopes, Marx told him, . . . never leads to the emancipation of such poor devils, but to their destruction . . . all you do by such methods is to ruin the very cause to which you have put your hand."

The reason why Marx and Engels were always clear that a fundamental change was unlikely to be peaceful, was given with clarity by the French historian, Mignet, in the introduction to the *History of the French Revolution* that he published in 1824. "When a reform has become necessary, and the moment for accomplishing it has arrived," he wrote, "nothing can prevent it, everything furthers it. Happy were it for men could they then come to an understanding; would the rich resign their superfluity, and the poor content themselves with achieving what they really needed, historians would have no excesses, no calamities, to record; he would merely have to display the transition of humanity to a wiser, freer and happier condition. But the annals of nations have not as yet presented any instance of such prudent sacrifices; those who should have made them have refused to do so; those who have required them have forcibly compelled them; and good has been brought about, like evil, by the medium, and with all the violence of usurpation. As yet, there has been no sovereign but force."

Mignet was not a socialist historian. Yet here, a quarter of a century before the *Communist Manifesto,* is one of the basic principles round which Marx and Engels built their social philosophy. Like them, Mignet recognised that at certain periods of history changes are necessary, and that if they are resisted they will impose themselves by violence. Like them also Mignet perceived that the changes which become necessary are independent of the views of those who are compelled to face them; and that it is rare indeed for those whom they affect adversely to offer them a welcome. Nevertheless, as he agreed, where such a situation has arrived violent revolution may bring with it good in its train. The usurpation of the power of a possessing class is, at such vital times, the source of well-being in society.

That is the theme of the *Communist Manifesto*. What it brought into social philosophy were four new and vital insights. It related, first, the need for inevitable change to the causes which made it inevitable. It linked that change, in the second place, to those divisions in the social order the antagonism between which has been the vital source of conflict between men. It explained, thirdly, why there was reason to suppose that the conflict between the dying capitalist way of life, and the emerging socialist way, would be the last stage in those conflicts, due to social division, and why, as they ended, there would begin a new and richer relation between man and man, since there would be, at long last, the final destruction of those fetters upon production which stood between humanity and its mastery of nature. Finally, the authors showed how men may become conscious of the historical position they occupy, and gather thereupon the knowledge that is necessary to take the next effective step upon the road of their long journey to freedom.

# IX

Few documents in the history of mankind have stood up so remarkably to the test of verification by the future as the *Communist Manifesto*. A century after its publication no one has been able seriously to controvert any of its major positions. All over the world the crises of capitalism have grown both more frequent and more profound. The fact that America has reached its last internal frontier has brought into being there precisely the same problems, if on a vaster scale, as in Europe, and the rising nationalisms of the Far East and the Pacific, while they hasten the decay of capitalism in the older industrial societies, quite obviously prelude their rise in the new. For, unmistakably, whether in Japan or China, whether in India or Indonesia, the central problem is the sheer misery of the masses; and our experience makes it clear that, within a capitalist framework, there is little likelihood of its effective mitigation. Nor is anyone likely to look at the prospect either in Latin America or in Africa and conclude that in either continent the business of government is carried on with the consent, or for the good, of the governed. Vice in both may pay to virtue the homage of occasional hypocrisy, but, in the intervals between those tributes, the squalor and vigour with which the many are exploited by the few, have changed less their character than the rhetoric under which they seek to conceal themselves.

But it is in Europe, above all, that the principles of the *Communist Manifesto* have found their fullest vindication by far. It is not only that even after two world wars fought in the name of democracy and freedom each of them has either perished altogether, or is in grave danger; it has been shown that, whereas in Great Britain and Scandinavia, deep historical traditions give to democracy and freedom an exceptional strength, the regard of the Right for their form is greater than their regard for their substance. The British Labour Party won a notable electoral victory at the close of the second World War. It has thus embarked upon the tremendous task of beginning to build the foundations of a socialist society in Great Britain in a period when, a large part of Europe having been devastated by war and the resources of the victorious powers, like Great Britain itself, drained almost to breaking-point, its task, both as a Socialist Party, and as a Government, is to ask for the continuance of great sacrifices from a people fatigued by the immense effort of war. To keep its authority, as Mr. Attlee himself has said,[1] "the Labour programme must be carried out with the utmost vigour and resolution. To delay dealing with essentials would be fatal. To show irresolution or cowardice would be to invite defeat. A Labour Government should make it quite plain that it will suffer nothing to hinder it in carrying out the popular will. In all great enterprises it is the first steps that are difficult, and it is the way in which these are taken

[1] *The Labour Party in Perspective* (London, 1937).

that makes the difference between success and failure."

It is not, I think merely patriotic emotion that
makes British socialists feel that here, as nowhere
else, the truth of their principles will be tested. It
was in Great Britain that capitalist society first came
to full maturity in the generation subsequent to the
Napoleonic Wars. It was largely from the observation and analysis of that maturity that Marxism
became the outstanding philosophic expression of
socialist principles and methods; and it was largely
from British socialist writers, and the early British
socialist movement, alike on its political and on its
trade union side, that Marx and Engels moved to
the understanding that men make their history by
their power, through their grasp of the forces which
make it move, to give a conscious direction to that
movement. Mr. Attlee has never been himself a
Marxist; but there is not a word in the sentences of
his that I have quoted which could not have been
eagerly accepted by the authors of the *Communist
Manifesto*; and they would, I think, have inferred
from them that in the degree to which the first Labour Government with a majority puts the spirit of
those phrases into operation, it would fulfil the great
objectives for which it was formed. By unbreakable
loyalty to its own principles it could lead its own
people, even in the hour of crisis, to cast off its
chains. A British working class that had achieved its
own emancipation could build that working-class
unity everywhere out of which the new world will finally be won.

# MANIFESTO OF THE COMMUNIST PARTY

# *Manifesto of the Communist Party*

## *I* • PREFACE TO THE GERMAN EDITION OF 1872

THE COMMUNIST LEAGUE, an international association of workers, which could of course be only a secret one, under the conditions obtaining at the time, commissioned us, the undersigned, at the Congress held in London in November, 1847, to write for publication a detailed theoretical and practical programme of the Party. Such was the origin of the following *Manifesto*, the manuscript of which travelled to London to be printed a few weeks before the February Revolution. First published in German, it has been republished in that language in at least twelve different editions in Germany, England and America. It was published in English for the first time in 1850 in the *Red Republican*, London, translated by Miss Helen Macfarlane, and in 1871 in at least three different translations in America. The French version first appeared in Paris shortly before the June insurrection of 1848, and recently in *Le Socialiste* of New York. A new translation is in the course of preparation. A Polish version appeared in London shortly after it was first published in German. A Russian translation was published in Geneva in the 'sixties. Into Danish, too, it was translated shortly after its first appearance.

However much the state of things may have altered during the last twenty-five years, the general principles laid down in this *Manifesto* are, on the whole, as correct to-day as ever. Here and there some detail might be improved. The practical application of the principles will depend, as the *Manifesto* itself states, everywhere and at all times, on the historical conditions for the time being existing, and, for that reason, no special stress is laid on the revolutionary measures proposed at the end of Section II. That passage would, in many respects, be very differently worded to-day. In view of the gigantic strides of modern industry since 1848, and of the accompanying improved and extended organisation of the working class, in view of the practical experience gained, first in the February Revolution, and then, still more, in the Paris Commune, where the proletariat for the first time held political power for two whole months, this programme has in some details become antiquated. One thing especially was proved by the Commune, viz., that "the working class cannot simply lay hold of the ready-made state machinery, and wield it for its own purposes." (See *The Civil War in France; Address of the General Council of the International Working Men's Association,* 1871, where this point is further developed.) Further, it is self-evident that the criticism of socialist literature is deficient in relation to the present time, because it comes down only to 1847; also that the remarks on the relation of the Communists to the various opposition parties (Section IV), although in principle still correct, yet in practice are antiquated, because the political situation has been entirely changed, and the progress of history has swept from off the earth the greater portion of the political parties there enumerated.

But then, the *Manifesto* has become a historical document which we have no longer any right to alter. A subsequent edition may perhaps appear with an introduction bridging the gap from 1847 to the present day; but this reprint was too unexpected to leave us time for that.

KARL MARX.   FREDERICK ENGELS

*London, 24 June, 1872*

# II • PREFACE TO THE RUSSIAN EDITION OF 1882

The first Russian edition of the *Manifesto of the Communist Party*, translated by Bakunin, was published early in the 'sixties by the printing office of the *Kolokol*. Then the West could see in it (the Russian edition of the *Manifesto*) only a literary curiosity. Such a view would be impossible to-day.

What a limited field the proletarian movement occupied at that time (December, 1847) is most clearly shown by the last section: the position of the Communists in relation to the various opposition parties in the various countries. Precisely Russia and the United States are missing here. It was the time when Russia constituted the last great reserve of all European reaction, when the United States absorbed the surplus proletarian forces of Europe through immigration. Both countries provided Europe with raw materials and were at the same time markets for the sale of its industrial products. Both were therefore, in one way or another, pillars of the existing European system.

How very different to-day. Precisely European immigration fitted North America for a gigantic agricultural production, whose competition is shaking the very foundations of European landed property—large and small. At the same time it enabled the United States to exploit its tremendous industrial resources with an energy and on a scale that must shortly break the industrial monopoly of Western Europe, and especially of England, existing up to now. Both circumstances react in a revolutionary manner upon America itself. Step by step the small and middle land ownership of the farmers, the basis of the whole political constitution, is succumbing to the competition of giant farms; at the same time a mass industrial proletariat and a fabulous concentration of capital funds are developing for the first time in the industrial regions.

And now Russia! During the Revolution of 1848–49 not only the European princes, but the European bourgeois as well, found their only salvation from the proletariat just beginning to awaken in Russian intervention. The Tsar was proclaimed the chief of European reaction. To-day he is a prisoner of war of the revolution in Gatchina, and Russia forms the vanguard of revolutionary action in Europe.

The *Communist Manifesto* had as its object the proclamation of the inevitable impending dissolution of modern bourgeois property. But in Russia we find, face to face with the rapidly flowering capitalist swindle and bourgeois property, just beginning to develop, more than half the land owned in common by the peasants. Now the question is: can the Russian *obshchina*, though greatly undermined, yet a form of the primaeval common ownership of land, pass directly to the higher form of Communist common ownership? Or on the contrary, must it first pass through the same process of dissolution such as constitutes the historical evolution of the West?

The only answer to that possible to-day is this: If the Russian Revolution becomes the signal for a proletarian revolution in the West, so that both complement each other, the present Russian common ownership of land may serve as the starting point for a communist development.

KARL MARX.   FREDERICK ENGELS

*London, 21 January, 1882.*

# III • PREFACE TO THE GERMAN EDITION OF 1883

The preface to the present edition I must, alas, sign alone. Marx, the man to whom the whole working class of Europe and America owes more than to any one else—rests at Highgate cemetery and over his grave the first grass is already growing. Since his death, there can be even less thought of revising or supplementing the *Manifesto*. But I consider it all the more necessary again to state the following expressly:

The basic thought running through the *Manifesto*—that economic production and the structure of society of every historical epoch necessarily arising therefrom constitute the foundation for the political and intellectual history of that epoch; that consequently (ever since the dissolution of the primaeval communal ownership of land) all history has been a history of class struggles, of struggles between exploited and exploiting, between dominated and dominating classes at various stages of social evolution; that this struggle, however, has now reached a stage where the exploited and oppressed class (the proletariat) can no longer emancipate itself from the class which exploits and oppresses it (the bourgeoisie), without at the same time forever freeing the whole of society from exploitation, oppression and class struggles—this basic thought belongs solely and exclusively to Marx.[1]

I have already stated this many times; but pre-

[1] "This proposition," I wrote in the preface to the English translation, "which, in my opinion, is destined to do for history what Darwin's theory has done for biology, we, both of us, had been gradually approaching for some years before 1845. How far I had independently progressed towards it is best shown by my *Condition of the Working Class in England*. But when I again met Marx at Brussels, in spring, 1845, he had it already worked out, and put it before me, in terms almost as clear as those in which I have stated it here." [*Note by F. Engels.*]

cisely now is it necessary that it also stand in front of the *Manifesto* itself.

FREDERICK ENGELS

*London, 28 June 1883.*

## IV • PREFACE TO THE GERMAN EDITION OF 1890

Since the above was written, a new German edition of the *Manifesto* has again become necessary, and much has also happened to the *Manifesto* which should be recorded here.

A second Russian translation—by Vera Zasulich—appeared at Geneva in 1882; the preface to that edition was written by Marx and myself. Unfortunately, the original German manuscript has gone astray; I must therefore re-translate from the Russian which will in no way improve the text. It reads:

"The first Russian edition of the *Manifesto of the Communist Party*, in Bakunin's translation, was published early in the 'sixties by the printing offices of the *Kolokol*. At that date a Russian edition of the *Manifesto* had for the West the significance, at most, of a literary curiosity. To-day such a view is no longer possible. How limited the area of the spread of the proletarian movement was at the time the *Manifesto* was first published (January, 1848) is best shown by the last section, *The Position of the Communists in Relation to the Various Opposition*

*Parties.* Russia and the United States above all are
missing. It was the time when Russia constituted the
last great reserve of European reaction and when
emigration to the United States absorbed the surplus
forces of the European proletariat. Both countries
provided Europe with raw materials, and served at
the same time as markets for the sale of its industrial
products. Both appeared therefore, in one way or
another, as pillars of the European social order.

"What a change has taken place since then! Precisely European emigration has made possible the
gigantic growth of agriculture in North America,
which through its competition is shaking the very
foundations of great and small landed property in
Europe. At the same time it enabled the United
States to begin the exploitation of its abundant industrial resources, and with such energy and on
such a scale that in a short time it must put an end
to the industrial monopoly of Western Europe.
These two circumstances react in turn upon America
in a revolutionary sense. More and more the small
and middle land ownership of the independent
farmers, the basis of the whole political system of
America, is succumbing to the competition of giant
farms, while simultaneously a numerous proletariat
is emerging for the first time in the industrial regions
alongside a fabulous concentration of capital.

"Let us now turn to Russia. At the time of the
Revolution of 1848–49, not only the European
monarchs, but the European bourgeois as well,
looked upon Russian intervention as the only salvation from the proletariat, then for the first time becoming aware of its own strength. The Tsar was
acclaimed the leader of European reaction. To-day

he sits in Gatchina, a prisoner of war of the revolution, and Russia forms the vanguard of the revolutionary movement in Europe.

"The object of the *Communist Manifesto* was to proclaim the inevitable impending downfall of present-day bourgeois property. But in Russia we find—side by side with the feverishly growing capitalist system and the bourgeois land ownership just beginning to take shape—more than half the land owned in common by the peasant.

"Now the question is: can the Russian peasant community, this form of primaeval common ownership of land, although already very much disintegrated, pass directly to a higher communist form of land ownership or must it first pass through the same process of dissolution represented in the historical evolution of the west?

"The only answer to this question possible to-day is the following. If the Russian Revolution becomes the signal for a workers' revolution in the West, so that both complement each other, the present Russian common ownership of land may then serve as the starting point for a communist development.

"London, 21 January 1882."

At about the same date, a new Polish version appeared in Geneva: *Manifest Kommunistyczny.*

Furthermore, a new Danish translation has appeared in the *Socialdemokratisk Bibliothek*, Copenhagen, 1885. Unfortunately it is not quite complete; certain essential passages, which seem to have presented difficulties to the translator, have been omitted and in addition there are signs of carelessness here and there, which are all the more unpleasantly conspicuous since the translation indicates that had the translator taken a little more pains he would have done an excellent piece of work.

A new French version appeared in 1886 in *Le Socialiste* of Paris; it is the best published to date.

From this latter a Spanish version was published the same year in *El Socialista* of Madrid, and then reissued in pamphlet form: *Manifesto del Partido Communista* por Carlos Marx y F. Engels, Madrid, Administracion de El Socialista, Hernan Cortes 8.

As a matter of curiosity I may mention that in 1887 the manuscript of an Armenian translation was offered to a publisher in Constantinople. But the good man did not have the courage to publish something bearing the name of Marx and suggested that the translator set down his own name as author, which the latter however declined.

After one and then another of the more or less inaccurate American translations had been repeatedly reprinted in England, an authentic version at last appeared in 1888. This was by my friend Samuel Moore and we went through it together once more before it was sent to press. It is entitled: *Manifesto of the Communist Party*, by Karl Marx and Frederick Engels. Authorised English translation, edited and annotated by Frederick Engels, 1888, London, William Reeves, 185 Fleet Street, E.C. I have added some of the notes of that edition to the present one.

The *Manifesto* has had a history of its own. Greeted with enthusiasm, at the time of its appearance, by the not at all numerous vanguard of scientific socialism (as is proved by the translations mentioned in the first preface), it was soon forced into the background by the reaction that began with the defeat of the Paris workers in June, 1848, and was finally excommunicated "by law" in the conviction of the Cologne Communists in November, 1852. With the disappearance from the public scene of the workers' movement that had begun with the February Revolution, the *Manifesto* too passed into the background.

When the European workers had again gathered sufficient strength for a new onslaught upon the power of the ruling classes, the International Working Men's Association came into being. Its aim was to weld together into *one* huge army the whole militant working class of Europe and America. Therefore it could not *set out* from the principles laid down in the *Manifesto*. It was bound to have a programme which would not shut the door on the English trade unions, the French, Belgian, Italian, and Spanish Proudhonists and the German Lassalleans. This programme—the considerations underlying the Statutes of the International—was drawn up by Marx with a master hand acknowledged even by Bakunin and the anarchists. For the ultimate final triumph of the ideas set forth in the *Manifesto*, Marx relied solely upon the intellectual development of the working class, as it necessarily has to ensue from united action and discussion. The events and vicissitudes in the struggle against capital, the defeats even more than the successes, could not but demonstrate to the fighters the inadequacy of their former universal panaceas and make their minds more receptive to a thorough understanding of the true conditions for working-class emancipation. And Marx was right. The working class of 1874, at the dissolution of the International, was altogether different from that of 1864, at its foundation. Proudhonism in the Latin countries and the specific Lassalleanism in Germany were dying out, and even the then arch-conservative English trade unions were gradually approaching the point where in 1887 the chairman of their Swansea Congress could say in their name: "Continental socialism has lost its terrors for us." Yet by 1887 continental socialism was almost exclusively the theory heralded in the *Manifesto*. Thus, to a certain extent, the history of the *Manifesto* reflects the history of the modern working-class movement since 1848. At present it is doubtless the most widely circulated, the most international product of all socialist literature, the common programme of many millions of workers of all countries from Siberia to California.

Nevertheless, when it appeared we could not have called it a *socialist* manifesto. In 1847 two kinds of people were considered socialists. On one hand were the adherents of the various utopian systems, notably the Owenites in England and the Fourierists in France, both of whom at that date had already dwindled to mere sects gradually dying out. On the other, the manifold types of social quacks who wanted to eliminate social abuses through their various universal panaceas and all kinds of patch-work, without hurting capital and profit in the least. In both cases, people who stood outside the labour movement and who looked for support rather to the "educated" classes. The section of the working class, however, which demanded a radical reconstruction of society, convinced that mere political revolutions were not enough, then called itself *Communist*. It was still a rough-hewn, only instinctive and frequently somewhat crude communism. Yet it was powerful enough to bring into being two systems of utopian communism—in France the "Icarian" communism of Cabet, and in Germany that of Weitling. Socialism in 1847 signified a bourgeois movement, communism a working-class movement. Socialism was, on the Continent at least, quite respectable, whereas communism was the very opposite. And since we were very decidedly of the opinion as early as then that "the emancipation of the workers must be the task of the working class itself," we could have no hesitation as to which of the two names we should choose. Nor has it ever occurred to us to repudiate it.

"Working men of all countries, unite!" But few voices responded when we proclaimed these words to the world forty-two years ago, on the eve of the first Paris Revolution in which the proletariat came out with the demands of its own. On 28 September 1864, however, the proletarians of most of the Western European countries joined hands in the International Working Men's Association of glorious memory. True, the International itself lived only nine years. But that the eternal union of the proletarians of all countries created by it is still alive and lives stronger than ever, there is no better witness than this day. Because to-day, as I write these lines, the European and American proletariat is reviewing its fighting forces, mobilised for the first time, mobilised as *one* army, under *one* flag, for *one* immediate aim: the standard eight-hour working day to be established by legal enactment, as proclaimed by the Geneva Congress of the International in 1866, and again by the Paris Workers' Congress in 1889. And to-day's spectacle will open the eyes of the capitalists and landlords of all countries to the fact that to-day the proletarians of all countries are united indeed.

If only Marx were still by my side to see this with his own eyes!

FREDERICK ENGELS

*London, 1 May 1890.*

# *V* • PREFACE TO THE ENGLISH EDITION OF 1888

The *Manifesto* was published as the platform of the Communist League, a working-men's association, first exclusively German, later on international, and, under the political conditions of the Continent before 1848, unavoidably a secret society. At a Congress of the League, held in November, 1847, Marx and Engels were commissioned to prepare for publication a complete theoretical and practical party programme. Drawn up in German, in January, 1848, the manuscript was sent to the printer in London a few weeks before the French revolution of 24 February. A French translation was brought out in Paris shortly before the insurrection of June, 1848. The first English translation, by Miss Helen Macfarlane, appeared in George Julian Harney's

*Red Republican*, London, 1850. A Danish and a Polish edition had also been published.

The defeat of the Parisian insurrection of June, 1848—the first great battle between proletariat and bourgeoisie—drove again into the background, for a time, the social and political aspirations of the European working class. Thenceforth, the struggle for supremacy was again, as it had been before the Revolution of February, solely between different sections of the propertied class; the working class was reduced to a fight for political elbow-room, and to the position of extreme wing of the middle-class Radicals. Wherever independent proletarian movements continued to show signs of life, they were ruthlessly hunted down. Thus the Prussian police hunted out the Central Board of the Communist League then located in Cologne. The members were arrested, and, after eighteen months' imprisonment, they were tried in October, 1852. This celebrated "Cologne Communist Trial" lasted from 4 October till 12 November; seven of the prisoners were sentenced to terms of imprisonment in a fortress, varying from three to six years. Immediately after the sentence the League was formally dissolved by the remaining members. As to the *Manifesto*, it seemed thenceforth to be doomed to oblivion.

When the European working class had recovered sufficient strength for another attack on the ruling classes, the International Working Men's Association sprang up. But this association, formed with the express aim of welding into one body the whole militant proletariat of Europe and America, could not at once proclaim the principles laid down in the *Manifesto*. The International was bound to have a programme broad enough to be acceptable to the English trade unions, to the followers of Proudhon in France, Belgium, Italy, and Spain, and to the Lassalleans[1] in Germany. Marx, who drew up this programme to the satisfaction of all parties, entirely trusted to the intellectual development of the working class, which was sure to result from combined action and mutual discussion. The very events and vicissitudes of the struggle against capital, the defeats even more than the victories, could not help bringing home to men's minds the insufficiency of their various favourite nostrums, and preparing the way for a more complete insight into the true conditions of working-class emancipation. And Marx was right. The International, on its breaking up in 1874, left the workers quite different men from what it had found them in 1864. Proudhonism in France, Lassalleanism in Germany were dying out, and even the conservative English trade unions, though most of them had long since severed their connection with the International, were gradually advancing towards that point at which, last year at Swansea, their president could say in their name: "Continental socialism has lost its terrors for us." In fact, the principles of the *Manifesto* had made considerable headway among the working men of all countries.

The *Manifesto* itself thus came to the front again. Since 1850 the German text had been reprinted

---

[1] Lassalle personally, to us, always acknowledged himself to be a disciple of Marx, and, as such, stood on the ground of the *Manifesto*. But in his public agitation, 1862–64, he did not go beyond demanding co-operative workshops supported by state credit. [*Note by F. Engels.*]

several times in Switzerland, England, and America. In 1872 it was translated into English in New York, where the translation was published in *Woodhull and Claflin's Weekly*. From this English version a French one was made in *Le Socialiste* of New York. Since then at least two more English translations, more or less mutilated, have been brought out in America, and one of them has been reprinted in England. The first Russian translation, made by Bakunin, was published at Herzen's *Kolokol* office in Geneva, about 1863; a second one, by the heroic Vera Zasulich, also in Geneva, in 1882. A new Danish edition is to be found in *Socialdemokratisk Bibliothek*, Copenhagen, 1885; a fresh French translation in *Le Socialiste*, Paris, 1886. From this latter, a Spanish version was prepared and published in Madrid, in 1886. The German reprints are not to be counted; there have been twelve altogether at the least. An Armenian translation, which was to be published in Constantinople some months ago, did not see the light, I am told, because the publisher was afraid of bringing out a book with the name of Marx on it, while the translator declined to call it his own production. Of further translations into other languages I have heard but had not seen. Thus the history of the *Manifesto* reflects, to great extent, the history of the modern working-class movement; at present it is undoubtedly the most wide spread, the most international production of all socialist literature, the common platform acknowledged by millions of working men from Siberia to California.

Yet, when it was written, we could not have called it a *socialist* manifesto. By Socialists, in 1847, were understood, on the one hand the adherents of the various Utopian systems: Owenites in England, Fourierists in France, both of them already reduced to the position of mere sects, and gradually dying out; on the other hand, the most multifarious social quacks, who by all manner of tinkering, professed to redress, without any danger to capital and profit, all sorts of social grievances, in both cases men outside the working-class movement, and looking rather to the "educated" classes for support. Whatever portion of the working class had become convinced of the insufficiency of mere political revolutions, and had proclaimed the necessity of a total social change, called itself Communist. It was a crude, rough-hewn, purely instinctive sort of communism; still it touched the cardinal point and was powerful enough amongst the working class to produce the Utopian communism of Cabet in France, and of Weitling in Germany. Thus, in 1847, socialism was a middle-class movement, communism a working-class movement. Socialism was, on the Continent at least, "respectable"; communism was the very opposite. And as our notion, from the very beginning, was that "the emancipation of the working class must be the act of the working class itself," there could be no doubt as to which of the two names we must take. Moreover, we have, ever since, been far from repudiating it.

The *Manifesto* being our joint production, I consider myself bound to state that the fundamental proposition which forms its nucleus belongs to Marx. That proposition is: That in every historical epoch, the prevailing mode of economic production and exchange, and the social organisation necessarily fol-

lowing from it, form the basis upon which is built
up, and from which alone can be explained the political and intellectual history of that epoch; that
consequently the whole history of mankind (since
the dissolution of primitive tribal society, holding
land in common ownership) has been a history of
class struggles, contests between exploiting and exploited, ruling and oppressed classes; that the history of these class struggles forms a series of
evolutions in which, nowadays, a stage has been
reached where the exploited and oppressed class—
the proletariat—cannot attain its emancipation from
the sway of the exploiting and ruling class—the bourgeoisie—without, at the same time, and once and for
all emancipating society at large from all exploitation, oppression, class distinction and class struggles.

This proposition, which, in my opinion, is destined
to do for history what Darwin's theory has done for
biology, we, both of us, had been gradually approaching for some years before 1845. How far I
had independently progressed towards it, is best
shown by my *Conditions of the Working Class in
England*. But when I again met Marx at Brussels, in
spring, 1845, he had it already worked out, and
put it before me, in terms almost as clear as those in
which I have stated it here.

From our joint preface to the German edition of
1872, I quote the following:

"However much the state of things may have altered during the last twenty-five years, the general
principles laid down in this *Manifesto* are, on the
whole, as correct to-day as ever. Here and there
some detail might be improved. The practical application of the principles will depend, as the

*Manifesto* itself states, everywhere and at all times, on the historical conditions for the time being existing, and, for that reason, no special stress is laid on the revolutionary measures proposed at the end of Section II. That passage would, in many respects, be very differently worked to-day. In view of the gigantic strides of modern industry since 1848, and of the accompanying improved and extended organisation of the working class, in view of the practical experience gained, first in the February Revolution, and then, still more, in the Paris Commune, where the proletariat for the first time held political power for two whole months, this programme has in some details become antiquated. One thing especially was proved by the Commune, viz., that 'the working class cannot simply lay hold of the ready-made state machinery, and wield it for its own purposes.' (See *The Civil War in France; Address of the General Council of the International Working Men's Association*, 1871, where this point is further developed.) Further, it is self-evident that the criticism of socialist literature is deficient in relation to the present time, because it comes down only to 1847; also, that the remarks on the relation of the Communists to the various opposition parties (Section IV), although in principle still correct, yet in practice are antiquated, because the political situation has been entirely changed, and the progress of history has swept from off the earth the greater portion of the political parties there enumerated.

"But then, the *Manifesto* has become a historical document which we have no longer any right to alter."

The present translation is by Mr. Samuel Moore,

the translator of the greater portion of Marx's *Capital*. We have revised it in common, and I have added a few notes explanatory of historical allusions.

FREDERICK ENGELS

*London, 30 January 1888.*

# Manifesto of
# the Communist Party

A SPECTRE is haunting Europe—the spectre of communism. All the powers of old Europe have entered into a holy alliance to exorcise this spectre: Pope and Tsar, Metternich and Guizot, French Radicals and German police-spies.

Where is the party in opposition that has not been decried as communistic by its opponents in power? Where is the opposition that has not hurled back the branding reproach of communism, against the more advanced opposition parties, as well as against its reactionary adversaries?

Two things result from this fact:

I. Communism is already acknowledged by all European powers to be itself a power.

II. It is high time that Communists should openly, in the face of the whole world, publish their views, their aims, their tendencies, and meet this nursery tale of the spectre of communism with a manifesto of the party itself.

To this end, Communists of various nationalities have assembled in London and sketched the following manifesto, to be published in the English, French, German, Italian, Flemish and Danish languages.

# *I* • BOURGEOIS AND PROLETARIANS[1]

The history of all hitherto existing society[2] is the history of class struggles.

Freeman and slave, patrician and plebeian, lord

---

[1] By bourgeoisie is meant the class of modern capitalists, owners of the means of social production and employers of wage labour. By proletariat, the class of modern wage labourers who, having no means of production of their own, are reduced to selling their labour power in order to live. [*Note by F. Engels to the English edition of* 1888.]

[2] That is, all *written* history. In 1847 the pre-history of society, the social organisation existing previous to recorded history, was all but unknown. Since then Haxthausen [August von, 1792–1866] discovered common ownership of land in Russia, Maurer [Georg Ludwig von] proved it to be the social foundation from which all Teutonic races started in history, and, by and by, village communities were found to be, or to have been, the primitive form of society everywhere from India to Ireland. The inner organisation of this primitive communistic society was laid bare, in its typical form, by Morgan's [Lewis Henry, 1818–81] crowning discovery of the true nature of the *gens* and its relation to the *tribe*. With the dissolution of these primaeval communities, society begins to be differentiated into separate and finally antagonistic classes. I have attempted to retrace this process of dissolution in *Der Ursprung der Familie, des Privateigenthums und des Staats* [*The Origin of the Family, Private Property and the State*], second edition, Stuttgart, 1886. [*Note by F. Engels to the English edition of* 1888.]

and serf, guild-master[8] and journeyman, in a word, oppressor and oppressed, stood in constant opposition to one another, carried on an uninterrupted, now hidden, now open fight, a fight that each time ended, either in a revolutionary reconstitution of society at large, or in the common ruin of the contending classes.

In the earlier epochs of history, we find almost everywhere a complicated arrangement of society into various orders, a manifold gradation of social rank. In ancient Rome we have patricians, knights, plebeians, slaves; in the Middle Ages, feudal lords, vassals, guild-masters, journeymen, apprentices, serfs; in almost all of these classes, again, subordinate gradations.

The modern bourgeois society that has sprouted from the ruins of feudal society has not done away with class antagonisms. It has but established new classes, new conditions of oppression, new forms of struggle in place of the old ones.

Our epoch, the epoch of the bourgeoisie, possesses, however, this distinctive feature: It has simplified the class antagonisms. Society as a whole is more and more splitting up into two great hostile camps, into two great classes directly facing each other—bourgeoisie and proletariat.

From the serfs of the Middle Ages sprang the chartered burghers of the earliest towns. From these burgesses the first elements of the bourgeoisie were developed.

The discovery of America, the rounding of the

[8] Guild-master, that is a full member of a guild, a master within, not a head of a guild. [*Note by F. Engels to the English edition of 1888.*]

Cape, opened up fresh ground for the rising bourgeoisie. The East-Indian and Chinese markets, the colonisation of America, trade with the colonies, the increase in the means of exchange and in commodities generally, gave to commerce, to navigation, to industry, an impulse never before known, and thereby, to the revolutionary element in the tottering feudal society, a rapid development.

The feudal system of industry, in which industrial production was monopolised by closed guilds, now no longer sufficed for the growing wants of the new markets. The manufacturing system took its place. The guild-masters were pushed aside by the manufacturing middle class; division of labour between the different corporate guilds vanished in the face of division of labour in each single workshop.

Meantime the markets kept ever growing, the demand ever rising. Even manufacture no longer sufficed. Thereupon, steam and machinery revolutionised industrial production. The place of manufacture was taken by the giant, modern industry, the place of the industrial middle class by industrial millionaires, the leaders of whole industrial armies, the modern bourgeois.

Modern industry has established the world market, for which the discovery of America paved the way. This market has given an immense development to commerce, to navigation, to communication by land. This development has, in its turn, reacted on the extension of industry; and in proportion as industry, commerce, navigation, railways extended, in the same proportion the bourgeoisie developed, increased its capital, and pushed into the background every class handed down from the Middle Ages.

We see, therefore, how the modern bourgeoisie is itself the product of a long course of development, of a series of revolutions in the modes of production and of exchange.

Each step in the development of the bourgeoisie was accompanied by a corresponding political advance of that class. An oppressed class under the sway of the feudal nobility, an armed and self-governing association in the medieval commune;[1] here independent urban republic (as in Italy and Germany), there taxable "third estate" of the monarchy (as in France); afterwards, in the period of manufacture proper, serving either the semi-feudal or the absolute monarchy as a counterpoise against the nobility, and, in fact, cornerstone of the great monarchies in general—the bourgeoisie has at last, since the establishment of modern industry and of the world market, conquered for itself, in the modern representative state, exclusive political sway. The executive of the modern state is but a committee for managing the common affairs of the whole bourgeoisie.

The bourgeoisie, historically, has played a most revolutionary part.

The bourgeoisie, wherever it has got the upper

[1] This was the name given their urban communities by the townsmen of Italy and France, after they had purchased or conquered their initial rights of self-government from their feudal lords. [*Note by F. Engels to the German edition of* 1890.]

"Commune" was the name taken in France by the nascent towns even before they had conquered from their feudal lords and masters local self-government and political rights as the "Third Estate". Generally speaking, for the economical development of the bourgeoisie, England is here taken as the typical country, for its political development, France. [*Note by F. Engels to the English edition of* 1888.]

hand, has put an end to all feudal, patriarchal, idyllic relations. It has pitilessly torn asunder the motley feudal ties that bound man to his "natural superiors," and has left no other nexus between man and man than naked self-interest, than callous "cash payment." It has drowned the most heavenly ecstasies of religious fervour, of chivalrous enthusiasm, of philistine sentimentalism, in the icy water of egotistical calculation. It has resolved personal worth into exchange value, and in place of the numberless indefeasible chartered freedoms, has set up that single, unconscionable freedom—Free Trade. In one word, for exploitation, veiled by religious and political illusions, it has substituted naked, shameless, direct, brutal exploitation.

The bourgeoisie has stripped of its halo every occupation hitherto honoured and looked up to with reverent awe. It has converted the physician, the lawyer, the priest, the poet, the man of science, into its paid wage labourers.

The bourgeoisie has torn away from the family its sentimental veil, and has reduced the family relation to a mere money relation.

The bourgeoisie has disclosed how it came to pass that the brutal display of vigour in the Middle Ages, which reactionaries so much admire, found its fitting complement in the most slothful indolence. It has been the first to show what man's activity can bring about. It has accomplished wonders far surpassing Egyptian pyramids, Roman aqueducts, and Gothic cathedrals; it has conducted expeditions that put in the shade all former exoduses of nations and crusades.

The bourgeoisie cannot exist without constantly

revolutionising the instruments of production, and thereby the relations of production, and with them the whole relations of society. Conservation of the old modes of production in unaltered form, was, on the contrary, the first condition of existence for all earlier industrial classes. Constant revolutionising of production, uninterrupted disturbance of all social conditions, everlasting uncertainty and agitation distinguish the bourgeois epoch from all earlier ones. All fixed, fast frozen relations, with their train of ancient and venerable prejudices and opinions, are swept away, all new-formed ones become antiquated before they can ossify. All that is solid melts into air, all that is holy is profaned, and man is at last compelled to face with sober senses his real conditions of life and his relations with his kind.

The need of a constantly expanding market for its products chases the bourgeoisie over the whole surface of the globe. It must nestle everywhere, settle everywhere, establish connections everywhere.

The bourgeoisie has through its exploitation of the world market given a cosmopolitan character to production and consumption in every country. To the great chagrin of reactionaries, it has drawn from under the feet of industry the national ground on which it stood. All old-established national industries have been destroyed or are daily being destroyed. They are dislodged by new industries, whose introduction becomes a life and death question for all civilised nations, by industries that no longer work up indigenous raw material, but raw material drawn from the remotest zones; industries whose products are consumed, not only at home, but in every quarter of the globe. In place of the old wants, satisfied by the production of the country, we find new wants, requiring for their satisfaction the products of distant lands and climes. In place of the old local and national seclusion and self-sufficiency, we have intercourse in every direction, universal inter-dependence of nations. And as in material, so also in intellectual production. The intellectual creations of individual nations become common property. National one-sidedness and narrow-mindedness become more and more impossible, and from the numerous national and local literatures there rises a world literature.

The bourgeoisie, by the rapid improvement of all instruments of production, by the immensely facilitated means of communication, draws all, even the most barbarian, nations into civilisation. The cheap prices of its commodities are the heavy artillery with which it batters down all Chinese walls, with which it forces the barbarians' intensely obstinate hatred of foreigners to capitulate. It compels all nations, on pain of extinction, to adopt the bourgeois mode of production; it compels them to introduce what it calls civilisation into their midst, i.e., to become bourgeois themselves. In one word, it creates a world after its own image.

The bourgeoisie has subjected the country to the rule of the towns. It has created enormous cities, has greatly increased the urban population as compared with the rural, and has thus rescued a considerable part of the population from the idiocy of rural life. Just as it has made the country dependent on the towns, so it has made barbarian and semi-barbarian countries dependent on the civilised ones, nations of peasants on nations of bourgeois, the East on the West.

The bourgeoisie keeps more and more doing away with the scattered state of the population, of the means of production, and of property. It has agglomerated population, centralised means of production, and has concentrated property in a few hands. The necessary consequence of this was political centralisation. Independent, or but loosely connected provinces, with separate interests, laws, governments, and systems of taxation, became lumped together into one nation, with one government, one code of laws, one national class interest, one frontier and one customs tariff.

The bourgeoisie, during its rule of scarce one hundred years, has created more massive and more colossal productive forces than have all preceding generations together. Subjection of nature's forces to man, machinery, application of chemistry to industry and agriculture, steam navigation, railways, electric telegraphs, clearing of whole continents for cultivation, canalisation of rivers, whole populations conjured out of the ground—what earlier century had even a presentiment that such productive forces slumbered in the lap of social labour?

We see then: the means of production and of exchange, on whose foundation the bourgeoisie built itself up, were generated in feudal society. At a certain stage in the development of these means of production and of exchange, the conditions under which feudal society produced and exchanged, the feudal organisation of agriculture and manufacturing industry, in one word, the feudal relations of property became no longer compatible with the already developed productive forces; they became so many fetters. They had to be burst asunder; they were burst asunder.

Into their place stepped free competition, accompanied by a social and political constitution adapted to it, and by the economic and political sway of the bourgeois class.

A similar movement is going on before our own eyes. Modern bourgeois society with its relations of production, of exchange and of property, a society that has conjured up such gigantic means of production and of exchange, is like the sorcerer who is no longer able to control the powers of the nether world whom he has called up by his spells. For many a decade past the history of industry and commerce is but the history of the revolt of modern productive forces against modern conditions of production, against the property relations that are the conditions for the existence of the bourgeoisie and of its rule. It is enough to mention the commercial crises that by their periodical return put the existence of the entire bourgeois society on its trial, each time more threateningly. In these crises a great part not only of the existing products, but also of the previously created productive forces, are periodically destroyed. In these crises there breaks out an epidemic that, in all earlier epochs, would have seemed an absurdity—the epidemic of over-production. Society suddenly finds itself put back into a state of momentary barbarism; it appears as if a famine, a universal war of devastation had cut off the supply of every means of subsistence; industry and commerce seem to be destroyed. And why? Because there is too much civilisation, too much means of subsistence, too much industry, too much commerce. The productive forces at the disposal of society no longer tend to further the development of the conditions of bourgeois property; on the contrary, they have become too powerful for these conditions, by which they are fettered, and so soon as they overcome these fetters, they bring disorder into the whole of bourgeois society, endanger the existence of bourgeois property. The conditions of bourgeois society are too narrow to comprise the wealth created by them. And how does the bourgeoisie get over these crises? On the one hand, by enforced destruction of a mass of productive forces; on the other, by the conquest of new markets, and by the more thorough exploitation of the old ones. That is to say, by paving the way for more extensive and more destructive crises, and by diminishing the means whereby crises are prevented.

The weapons with which the bourgeoisie felled feudalism to the ground are now turned against the bourgeoisie itself.

But not only has the bourgeoisie forged the weapons that bring death to itself; it has also called into existence the men who are to wield those weapons—the modern working class—the proletarians.

In proportion as the bourgeoisie, i.e., capital, is developed, in the same proportion is the proletariat, the modern working class, developed—a class of labourers, who live only so long as they find work, and who find work only so long as their labour increases capital. These labourers, who must sell themselves piecemeal, are a commodity, like every other article of commerce, and are consequently exposed to all the vicissitudes of competition, to all the fluctuations of the market.

Owing to the extensive use of machinery and to division of labour, the work of the proletarians has lost all individual character, and, consequently, all charm for the workman. He becomes an appendage of the machine, and it is only the most simple, most monotonous, and most easily acquired knack, that is required of him. Hence, the cost of production of a workman is restricted, almost entirely, to the means of subsistence that he requires for his maintenance, and for the propagation of his race. But the price of a commodity, and therefore also of labour, is equal to its cost of production. In proportion, therefore, as the repulsiveness of the work increases, the wage decreases. Nay more, in proportion as the use of machinery and division of labour increases, in the same proportion the burden of toil also increases, whether by prolongation of the working hours, by increase of the work exacted in a given time, or by increased speed of the machinery, etc.

Modern industry has converted the little workshop of the patriarchal master into the great factory of the industrial capitalist. Masses of labourers, crowded into the factory, are organised like soldiers. As privates of the industrial army they are placed under the command of a perfect hierarchy of officers and sergeants. Not only are they slaves of the bourgeois class, and of the bourgeois state; they are daily and hourly enslaved by the machine, by the overlooker, and, above all, by the individual bourgeois manufacturer himself. The more openly this despotism proclaims gain to be its end and aim, the more petty, the more hateful and the more embittering it is.

The less the skill and exertion of strength implied in manual labour, in other words, the more modern industry becomes developed, the more is the labour of men superseded by that of women. Differences of age and sex have no longer any distinctive social validity for the working class. All are instruments of labour, more or less expensive to use, according to their age and sex.

No sooner is the exploitation of the labourer by the manufacturer, so far at an end, that he receives his wages in cash, than he is set upon by the other portions of the bourgeoisie, the landlord, the shopkeeper, the pawnbroker, etc.

The lower strata of the middle class—the small tradespeople, shopkeepers, and retired tradesmen generally, the handicraftsmen and peasants—all these sink gradually into the proletariat, partly because their diminutive capital does not suffice for the scale on which modern industry is carried on, and is swamped in the competition with the large capitalists, partly because their specialised skill is rendered worthless by new methods of production. Thus the proletariat is recruited from all classes of the population.

The proletariat goes through various stages of development. With its birth begins its struggle with the bourgeoisie. At first the contest is carried on by individual labourers, then by the work people of a factory, then by the operatives of one trade, in one locality, against the individual bourgeois who directly exploits them. They direct their attacks not against the bourgeois conditions of production, but against the instruments of production themselves; they destroy imported wares that compete with their labour, they smash to pieces machinery, they set factories ablaze, they seek to restore by force the vanished status of the workman of the Middle Ages.

At this stage the labourers still form an incoherent mass scattered over the whole country, and broken up by their mutual competition. If anywhere they unite to form more compact bodies, this is not yet the consequence of their own active union, but of the union of the bourgeoisie, which class, in order to attain its own political ends, is compelled to set the whole proletariat in motion, and is moreover yet, for a time, able to do so. At this stage, therefore, the proletarians do not fight their enemies, but the enemies of their enemies, the remnants of absolute monarchy, the landowners, the non-industrial bourgeois, the petty bourgeoisie. Thus the whole historical movement is concentrated in the hands of the bourgeoisie; every victory so obtained is a victory for the bourgeoisie.

But with the development of industry the proletariat not only increases in number; it becomes concentrated in greater masses, its strength grows, and it feels that strength more. The various interests and conditions of life within the ranks of the proletariat are more and more equalised, in proportion as machinery obliterates all distinctions of labour, and nearly everywhere reduces wages to the same low level. The growing competition among the bourgeois, and the resulting commercial crises, make the wages of the workers ever more fluctuating. The unceasing improvement of machinery, ever more rapidly developing, makes their livelihood more and

more precarious; the collisions between individual
workmen and individual bourgeois take more and
more the character of collisions between two classes.
Thereupon the workers begin to form combinations
(trade unions) against the bourgeois; they club together in order to keep up the rate of wages; they
found permanent associations in order to make
provision beforehand for these occasional revolts.
Here and there the contest breaks out into riots.

Now and then the workers are victorious, but only
for a time. The real fruit of their battles lies, not in
the immediate result, but in the ever expanding
union of the workers. This union is helped on by the
improved means of communication that are created
by modern industry, and that place the workers of
different localities in contact with another. It was
just this contact that was needed to centralise the
numerous local struggles, all of the same character,
into one national struggle between classes. But every
class struggle is a political struggle. And that union,
to attain which the burghers of the Middle Ages,
with their miserable highways, required centuries,
the modern proletarians, thanks to railways, achieve
in a few years.

This organisation of the proletarians into a class,
and consequently into a political party, is continually being upset again by the competition between
the workers themselves. But it ever rises up again,
stronger, firmer, mightier. It compels legislative
recognition of particular interests of the workers, by
taking advantage of the divisions among the bourgeoisie itself. Thus the Ten-Hours Bill in England
was carried.

Altogether, collisions between the classes of the

old society further in many ways the course of development of the proletariat. The bourgeoisie finds itself involved in a constant battle. At first with the aristocracy; later on, with those portions of the bourgeoisie itself, whose interests have become antagonistic to the progress of industry; at all time with the bourgeoisie of foreign countries. In all these battles it sees itself compelled to appeal to the proletariat, to ask for its help, and thus, to drag it into the political arena. The bourgeoisie itself, therefore, supplies the proletariat with its own elements of political and general education, in other words, it furnishes the proletariat with weapons for fighting the bourgeoisie.

Further, as we have already seen, entire sections of the ruling classes are, by the advance of industry, precipitated into the proletariat, or are at least threatened in their conditions of existence. These also supply the proletariat with fresh elements of enlightenment and progress.

Finally, in times when the class struggle nears the decisive hour, the process of dissolution going on within the ruling class, in fact within the whole range of old society, assumes such a violent, glaring character, that a small section of the ruling class cuts itself adrift, and joins the revolutionary class, the class that holds the future in its hands. Just as, therefore, at an earlier period, a section of the nobility went over to the bourgeoisie, so now a portion of the bourgeoisie goes over to the proletariat, and in particular, a portion of the bourgeois ideologists, who have raised themselves to the level of comprehending theoretically the historical movement as a whole.

Of all the classes that stand face to face with the bourgeoisie to-day, the proletariat alone is a really revolutionary class. The other classes decay and finally disappear in the face of modern industry; the proletariat is its special and essential product.

The lower middle class, the small manufacturer, the shopkeeper, the artisan, the peasant, all these fight against the bourgeoisie, to save from extinction their existence as fractions of the middle class. They are therefore not revolutionary, but conservative. Nay, more, they are reactionary, for they try to roll back the wheel of history. If by chance they are revolutionary, they are so only in view of their impending transfer into the proletariat; they thus defend not their present, but their future interests; they desert their own standpoint to place themselves at that of the proletariat.

The "dangerous class," the social scum, that passively rotting mass thrown off by the lowest layers of old society, may, here and there, be swept into the movement by a proletarian revolution; its conditions of life, however, prepare it far more for the part of a bribed tool of reactionary intrigue.

In the conditions of the proletariat, those of old society at large are already virtually swamped. The proletarian is without property; his relation to his wife and children has no longer anything in common with the bourgeois family relations; modern industrial labour, modern subjection to capital, the same in England as in France, in America as in Germany, has stripped him of every trace of national character. Law, morality, religion, are to him so many bourgeois prejudices, behind which lurk in ambush just as many bourgeois interests.

All the preceding classes that got the upper hand, sought to fortify their already acquired status by subjecting society at large to their conditions of appropriation. The proletarians cannot become masters of the productive forces of society, except by abolishing their own previous mode of appropriation, and thereby also every other previous mode of appropriation. They have nothing of their own to secure and to fortify; their mission is to destroy all previous securities for, and insurances of, individual property.

All previous historical movements were movements of minorities, or in the interest of minorities. The proletarian movement is the self-conscious, independent movement of the immense majority, in the interest of the immense majority. The proletariat, the lowest stratum of our present society, cannot stir, cannot raise itself up, without the whole superincumbent strata of official society being sprung into the air.

Though not in substance, yet in form, the struggle of the proletariat with the bourgeoisie is at first a national struggle. The proletariat of each country must, of course, first of all settle matters with its own bourgeoisie.

In depicting the most general phases of the development of the proletariat, we traced the more or less veiled civil war, raging within existing society, up to the point where that war breaks out into open revolution, and where the violent overthrow of the bourgeoisie lays the foundation for the sway of the proletariat.

Hitherto, every form of society has been based, as we have already seen, on the antagonism of oppressing and oppressed classes. But in order to oppress a class, certain conditions must be assured to it under which it can, at least, continue its slavish existence. The serf, in the period of serfdom, raised himself to membership in the commune, just as the petty bourgeois, under the yoke of feudal absolutism, managed to develop into a bourgeois. The modern labourer, on the contrary, instead of rising with the progress of industry, sinks deeper and deeper below the conditions of existence of his own class. He becomes a pauper, and pauperism develops more rapidly than population and wealth. And here it becomes evident that the bourgeoisie is unfit any longer to be the ruling class in society, and to impose its conditions of existence upon society as an overriding law. It is unfit to rule because it is incompetent to assure an existence to its slave within his slavery, because it cannot help letting him sink into such a state, that it has to feed him, instead of being fed by him. Society can no longer live under this bourgeoisie, in other words, its existence is no longer compatible with society.

The essential condition for the existence and for the sway of the bourgeois class, is the formation and augmentation of capital; the condition for capital is wage labour. Wage labour rests exclusively on competition between the labourers. The advance of industry, whose involuntary promoter is the bourgeoisie, replaces the isolation of the labourers, due to competition, by their revolutionary combination, due to association. The development of modern industry, therefore, cuts from under its feet the very foundation on which the bourgeoisie produces and appropriates products. What the bourgeoisie therefore produces, above all, are its own grave-diggers. Its fall and the victory of the proletariat are equally inevitable.

# II • PROLETARIANS AND COMMUNISTS

In what relation do the Communists stand to the proletarians as a whole?

The Communists do not form a separate party opposed to other working-class parties.

They have no interests separate and apart from those of the proletariat as a whole.

They do not set up any sectarian principles of their own, by which to shape and mould the proletarian movement.

The Communists are distinguished from the other working-class parties by this only: (1) In the national struggles of the proletarians of the different countries, they point out and bring to the front the common interests of the entire proletariat, independently of all nationality. (2) In the various stages of development which the struggle of the working class against the bourgeoisie has to pass through, they always and everywhere represent the interests of the movement as a whole.

The Communists, therefore, are on the one hand, practically, the most advanced and resolute section of the working-class parties of every country, that section which pushes forward all others; on the other hand, theoretically, they have over the great mass of the proletariat the advantage of clearly understanding the lines of march, the conditions, and the ultimate general results of the proletarian movement.

The immediate aim of the Communists is the same as that of all other proletarian parties: Formation of the proletariat into a class, overthrow of the bourgeois supremacy, conquest of political power by the proletariat.

The theoretical conclusions of the Communists are in no way based on ideas or principles that have been invented, or discovered, by this or that would-be universal reformer.

They merely express, in general terms, actual relations springing from an existing class struggle, from a historical movement going on under our very eyes. The abolition of existing property relations is not at all a distinctive feature of communism.

All property relations in the past have continually been subject to historical change consequent upon the change in historical conditions.

The French Revolution, for example, abolished feudal property in favour of bourgeois property.

The distinguishing feature of communism is not the abolition of property generally, but the abolition of bourgeois property. But modern bourgeois private property is the final and most complete expression of the system of producing and appropriating products that is based on class antagonisms, on the exploitation of the many by the few.

In this sense, the theory of the Communists may be summed up in the single sentence: Abolition of private property.

We Communists have been reproached with the

desire of abolishing the right of personally acquiring property as the fruit of a man's own labour, which property is alleged to be the groundwork of all personal freedom, activity and independence.

Hard-won, self-acquired, self-earned property! Do you mean the property of the petty artisan and of the small peasant, a form of property that preceded the bourgeois form? There is no need to abolish that; the development of industry has to a great extent already destroyed it, and it is still destroying it daily.

Or do you mean modern bourgeois private property?

But does wage labour create any property for the labourer? Not a bit. It creates capital, i.e., that kind of property which exploits wage labour, and which cannot increase except upon conditions of begetting a new supply of wage labour for fresh exploitation. Property, in its present form, is based on the antagonism of capital and wage labour. Let us examine both sides of this antagonism.

To be a capitalist, is to have not only a purely personal, but a social, *status* in production. Capital is a collective product, and only by the united action of many members, nay, in the last resort, only by the united action of all members of society, can it be set in motion.

Capital is therefore not a personal, it is a social power.

When, therefore, capital is converted into common property, into the property of all members of society, personal property is not thereby transformed into social property. It is only the social character of the property that is changed. It loses its class character.

Let us now take wage labour.

The average price of wage labour is the minimum wage, i.e., that quantum of the means of subsistence which is absolutely requisite to keep the labourer in bare existence as a labourer. What, therefore, the wage labourer appropriates by means of his labour, merely suffices to prolong and reproduce a bare existence. We by no means intend to abolish this personal appropriation of the products of labour, an appropriation that is made for the maintenance and reproduction of human life, and that leaves no surplus wherewith to command the labour of others. All that we want to do away with is the miserable character of this appropriation, under which the labourer lives merely to increase capital, and is allowed to live only in so far as the interest of the ruling class requires it.

In bourgeois society, living labour is but a means to increase accumulated labour. In communist society, accumulated labour is but a means to widen, to enrich, to promote the existence of the labourer.

In bourgeois society, therefore, the past dominates the present; in communist society, the present dominates the past. In bourgeois society capital is independent and has individuality, while the living person is dependent and has no individuality.

And the abolition of this state of things is called by the bourgeois, abolition of individuality and freedom! And rightly so. The abolition of bourgeois individuality, bourgeois independence, and bourgeois freedom is undoubtedly aimed at.

By freedom is meant, under the present bourgeois conditions of production, free trade, free selling and buying.

But if selling and buying disappears, free selling and buying disappears also. This talk about free selling and buying, and all the other "brave words" of our bourgeoisie about freedom in general, have a meaning, if any, only in contrast with restricted selling and buying, with the fettered traders of the Middle Ages, but have no meaning when opposed to the communist abolition of buying and selling, of the bourgeois conditions of production, and of the bourgeoisie itself.

You are horrified at our intending to do away with private property. But in your existing society, private property is already done away with for nine-tenths of the population; its existence for the few is solely due to its non-existence in the hands of those nine-tenths. You reproach us, therefore, with intending to do away with a form of property, the necessary condition for whose existence is the non-existence of any property for the immense majority of society.

In one word, you reproach us with intending to do away with your property. Precisely so; that is just what we intend.

From the moment when labour can no longer be converted into capital, money or rent, into a social power capable of being monopolised, i.e., from the moment when individual property can no longer be transformed into bourgeois property, into capital, from that moment, you say, individuality vanishes.

You must, therefore, confess that by "individual" you mean no other person than the bourgeois, than the middle-class owner of property. This person must, indeed, be swept out of the way, and made impossible.

Communism deprives no man of the power to appropriate the products of society; all that it does is to deprive him of the power to subjugate the labour of others by means of such appropriation.

It has been objected, that upon the abolition of private property all work will cease, and universal laziness will overtake us.

According to this, bourgeois society ought long ago to have gone to the dogs through sheer idleness; for those of its members who work, acquire nothing, and those who acquire anything, do not work. The whole of this objection is but another expression of the tautology: There can no longer be any wage labour when there is no longer any capital.

All objections urged against the communistic mode of producing and appropriating material products, have, in the same way, been urged against the communistic modes of producing and appropriating intellectual products. Just as to the bourgeois, the disappearance of class property is the disappearance of production itself, so the disappearance of class culture is to him identical with the disappearance of all culture.

That culture, the loss of which he laments, is, for the enormous majority, a mere training to act as a machine.

But don't wrangle with us so long as you apply, to our intended abolition of bourgeois property, the standard of your bourgeois notions of freedom, culture, law, etc. Your very ideas are but the outgrowth of the conditions of your bourgeois production and bourgeois property, just as your jurisprudence is but the will of your class made into a law for all, a will whose essential character and direction are determined by the economical conditions of existence of your class.

The selfish misconception that induces you to transform into eternal laws of nature and of reason, the social forms springing from your present mode of production and form of property—historical relations that rise and disappear in the progress of production—this misconception you share with every ruling class that has preceded you. What you see clearly in the case of ancient property, what you admit in the case of feudal property, you are of course forbidden to admit in the case of your own bourgeois form of property.

Abolition of the family! Even the most radical flare up at this infamous proposal of the Communists.

On what foundation is the present family, the bourgeois family, based? On capital, on private gain. In its completely developed form this family exists only among the bourgeoisie. But this state of things finds its complement in the practical absence of the family among proletarians, and in public prostitution.

The bourgeois family will vanish as a matter of course when its complement vanishes, and both will vanish with the vanishing of capital.

Do you charge us with wanting to stop the exploitation of children by their parents? To this crime we plead guilty.

But, you will say, we destroy the most hallowed of relations, when we replace home education by social.

And your education! Is not that also social, and determined by the social conditions under which you educate, by the intervention direct or indirect, of society, by means of schools, etc.? The Communists have not invented the intervention of society in education; they do but seek to alter the character of that intervention, and to rescue education from the influence of the ruling class.

The bourgeois claptrap about the family and education, about the hallowed correlation of parent and child, becomes all the more disgusting, the more, by the action of modern industry, all family ties among the proletarians are torn asunder, and their children transformed into simple articles of commerce and instruments of labour.

But you Communists would introduce community of women, screams the whole bourgeoisie in chorus.

The bourgeois sees in his wife a mere instrument of production. He hears that the instruments of production are to be exploited in common, and, naturally, can come to no other conclusion than that the lot of being common to all will likewise fall to the women.

He has not even a suspicion that the real point aimed at is to do away with the status of women as mere instruments of production.

For the rest, nothing is more ridiculous than the virtuous indignation of our bourgeois at the community of women which, they pretend, is to be openly and officially established by the Communists. The Communists have no need to introduce community of women; it has existed almost from time immemorial.

Our bourgeois, not content with having wives and daughters of their proletarians at their disposal, not to speak of common prostitutes, take the greatest pleasure in seducing each other's wives.

Bourgeois marriage is in reality a system of wives in common and thus, at the most, what the Communists might possibly be reproached with is that they desire to introduce, in substitution for a hypocritically concealed, an openly legalised community of women. For the rest, it is self-evident, that the abolition of the present system of production must bring with it the abolition of the community of women springing from that system, i.e., of prostitution both public and private.

The Communists are further reproached with desiring to abolish countries and nationality.

The working men have no country. We cannot take from them what they have not got. Since the proletariat must first of all acquire political supremacy, must rise to be the leading class of the nation, must constitute itself *the* nation, it is, so far, itself national, though not in the bourgeois sense of the word.

National differences and antagonism between peoples are daily more and more vanishing, owing to the development of the bourgeoisie, to freedom of commerce, to the world market, to uniformity in the mode of production and in the conditions of life corresponding thereto.

The supremacy of the proletariat will cause them to vanish still faster. United action of the leading civilised countries at least, is one of the first conditions for the emancipation of the proletariat.

In proportion as the exploitation of one individual by another is put an end to, the exploitation of one nation by another will also be put an end to. In proportion as the antagonism between classes within the nation vanishes, the hostility of one nation to another will come to an end.

The charges against communism made from a religious, a philosophical and, generally, from an ideological standpoint, are not deserving of serious examination.

Does it require deep intuition to comprehend that man's ideas, views, and conceptions, in one word, man's consciousness, changes with every change in the conditions of his material existence, in his social relations and in his social life?

What else does the history of ideas prove, than that intellectual production changes its character in proportion as material production is changed? The ruling ideas of each age have ever been the ideas of its ruling class.

When people speak of ideas that revolutionise society, they do but express the fact that within the old society the elements of a new one have been created, and that the dissolution of the old ideas keeps even pace with the dissolution of the old conditions of existence.

When the ancient world was in its last throes, the ancient religions were overcome by Christianity. When Christian ideas succumbed in the eighteenth century to rationalist ideas, feudal society fought its death battle with the then revolutionary bourgeoisie. The ideas of religious liberty and freedom of conscience, merely gave expression to the sway of free competition within the domain of knowledge.

"Undoubtedly," it will be said, "religious, moral, philosophical and juridical ideas have been modified in the course of historical development. But religion, morality, philosophy, political science, and law, constantly survived this change."

"There are, besides, eternal truths, such as Freedom, Justice, etc., that are common to all states of society. But communism abolishes eternal truths, it abolishes all religion, and all morality, instead of constituting them on a new basis; it therefore acts in contradiction to all past historical experience."

What does this accusation reduce itself to? The history of all past society has consisted in the development of class antagonisms, antagonisms that assumed different forms at different epochs.

But whatever form they may have taken, one fact is common to all past ages, viz., the exploitation of one part of society by the other. No wonder, then, that the social consciousness of past ages, despite all the multiplicity and variety it displays, moves within certain common forms, or general ideas, which cannot completely vanish except with the total disappearance of class antagonisms.

The communist revolution is the most radical rupture with traditional relations; no wonder that its development involves the most radical rupture with traditional ideas.

But let us have done with the bourgeois objections to communism.

We have seen above that the first step in the revolution by the working class is to raise the proletariat to the position of ruling class to win the battle of democracy.

The proletariat will use its political supremacy to wrest, by degrees, all capital from the bourgeoisie, to centralise all instruments of production in the hands of the state. i.e., of the proletariat organised as the ruling class; and to increase the total productive forces as rapidly as possible.

Of course, in the beginning, this cannot be effected except by means of despotic inroads on the rights of property, and on the conditions of bourgeois production; by means of measures, therefore, which appear economically insufficient and untenable, but which, in the course of the movement, outstrip themselves, necessitate further inroads upon the old social order, and are unavoidable as a means of entirely revolutionising the mode of production.

These measures will of course be different in different countries.

Nevertheless, in the most advanced countries, the following will be pretty generally applicable.

1. Abolition of property in land and application of all rents of land to public purposes.

2. A heavy progressive or graduated income tax.

3. Abolition of all right of inheritance.

4. Confiscation of the property of all emigrants and rebels.

5. Centralisation of credit in the hands of the state, by means of a national bank with state capital and an exclusive monopoly.

6. Centralisation of the means of communication and transport in the hands of the state.

7. Extension of factories and instruments of production owned by the state; the bringing into cultivation of waste lands, and the improvement of the soil generally in accordance with a common plan.

8. Equal obligation of all to work. Establishment of industrial armies, especially for agriculture.

9. Combination of agriculture with manufacturing industries; gradual abolition of all the distinction

between town and country by a more equable distribution of the population over the country.

10. Free education for all children in public schools. Abolition of children's factory labour in its present form. Combination of education with industrial production, etc.

When, in the course of development, class distinctions have disappeared, and all production has been concentrated in the hands of a vast association of the whole nation, the public power will lose its political character. Political power, properly so called, is merely the organised power of one class for oppressing another. If the proletariat during its contest with the bourgeoisie is compelled, by the force of circumstances, to organise itself as a class; if, by means of a revolution, it makes itself the ruling class, and, as such, sweeps away by force the old conditions of production, then it will, along with these conditions, have swept away the conditions for the existence of class antagonisms and of classes generally, and will thereby have abolished its own supremacy as a class.

In place of the old bourgeois society, with its classes and class antagonisms, we shall have an association in which the free development of each is the condition for the free development of all.

# *III* • SOCIALIST AND COMMUNIST LITERATURE

## 1. *REACTIONARY SOCIALISM*

### *a. Feudal Socialism*

Owing to their historical position it became the vocation of the aristocracies of France and England to write pamphlets against modern bourgeois society. In the French Revolution of July, 1830, and in the English reform agitation, these aristocracies again succumbed to the hateful upstart. Thenceforth a serious political struggle was altogether out of the question. A literary battle alone remained possible. But even in the domain of literature the old cries of the restoration period[1] had become impossible.

In order to arouse sympathy the aristocracy was obliged to lose sight, apparently, of its own interests, and to formulate its indictment against the bourgeoisie in the interest of the exploited working class alone. Thus the aristocracy took their revenge by singing lampoons on their new master and whispering in his ears sinister prophecies of coming catastrophe.

[1] Not the English Restoration, 1660 to 1689, but the French Restoration, 1814 to 1830. [*Note by F. Engels to the English edition of* 1888.]

In this way arose feudal socialism: half lamentation, half lampoon; half echo of the past, half menace of the future; at times, by its bitter, witty and incisive criticism, striking the bourgeoisie to the very heart's core, but always ludicrous in its effect, through total incapacity to comprehend the march of modern history.

The aristocracy, in order to rally the people to them, waved the proletarian alms-bag in front for a banner. But the people, so often as it joined them, saw on their hindquarters the old feudal coats of arms, and deserted with loud and irreverent laughter.

One section of the French Legitimists and "Young England" exhibited this spectacle.

In pointing out that their mode of exploitation was different to that of the bourgeoisie, the feudalists forget that they exploited under circumstances and conditions that were quite different and that are now antiquated. In showing that, under their rule, the modern proletariat never existed, they forget that the modern bourgeoisie is the necessary offspring of their own form of society.

For the rest, so little do they conceal the reactionary character of their criticism that their chief accusation against the bourgeoisie amounts to this, that under the bourgeois régime a class is being developed which is destined to cut up root and branch the old order of society.

What they upbraid the bourgeoisie with is not so much that it creates a proletariat as that it creates a *revolutionary* proletariat.

In political practice, therefore, they join in all coercive measures against the working class; and in ordinary life, despite their high falutin' phrases, they stoop to pick up the golden apples dropped from the tree of industry, and to barter truth, love, and honour for traffic in wool, beetroot-sugar, and potato spirits.[1]

As the parson has ever gone hand in hand with the landlord, so has clerical socialism with feudal socialism.

Nothing is easier than to give Christian asceticism a socialist tinge. Has not Christianity declaimed against private property, against marriage, against the state? Has it not preached in the place of these, charity and poverty, celibacy and mortification of the flesh, monastic life and Mother Church? Christian socialism is but the holy water with which the priest consecrates the heart-burnings of the aristocrat.

### b. Petty-Bourgeois Socialism

The feudal aristocracy was not the only class that was ruined by the bourgeoisie, not the only class whose conditions of existence pined and perished in the atmosphere of modern bourgeois society. The medieval burgesses and the small peasant proprietors were the precursors of the modern bourgeoisie. In those countries which are but little developed, in-

[1] This applies chiefly to Germany where the landed aristocracy and squirearchy have large portions of their estates cultivated for their own account by stewards, and are, moreover, extensive beetroot-sugar manufacturers and distillers of potato spirits. The wealthier British aristocracy are, as yet, rather above that; but they, too, know how to make up for declining rents by lending their names to floaters of more or less shady joint-stock companies. [*Note by F. Engels to the English edition of 1888.*]

dustrially and commercially, these two classes still vegetate side by side with the rising bourgeoisie.

In countries where modern civilisation has become fully developed, a new class of petty bourgeois has been formed, fluctuating between proletariat and bourgeoisie, and ever renewing itself as a supplementary part of bourgeois society. The individual members of this class, however, are being constantly hurled down into the proletariat by the action of competition, and, as modern industry develops, they even see the moment approaching when they will completely disappear as an independent section of modern society, to be replaced, in manufactures, agriculture and commerce, by overlookers, bailiffs and shopmen.

In countries like France, where the peasants constitute far more than half of the population, it was natural that writers who sided with the proletariat against the bourgeoisie should use, in their criticism of the bourgeois régime, the standard of the peasant and petty bourgeois, and from the standpoint of these intermediate classes should take up the cudgels for the working class. Thus arose petty-bourgeois socialism. Sismondi was the head of this school, not only in France but also in England.

This school of socialism dissected with great acuteness the contradictions in the conditions of modern production. It laid bare the hypocritical apologies of economists. It proved, incontrovertibly, the disastrous effects of machinery and division of labour; the concentration of capital and land in a few hands; overproduction and crises; it pointed out the inevitable ruin of the petty bourgeois and peasant, the misery of the proletariat, the anarchy in

MANIFESTO OF THE COMMUNIST PARTY

production, the crying inequalities in the distribution of wealth, the industrial war of extermination between nations, the dissolution of old moral bonds, of the old family relations, of the old nationalities.

In its positive aims, however, this form of socialism aspires either to restoring the old means of production and of exchange, and with them the old property relations, and the old society, or to cramping the modern means of production and of exchange within the framework of the old property relations that have been, and were bound to be, exploded by those means. In either case it is both reactionary and utopian.

Its last words are: Corporate guilds for manufacture; patriarchal relations in agriculture.

Ultimately, when stubborn historical facts had dispersed all intoxicating effects of self-deception, this form of socialism ended in a miserable fit of the blues.

### c. German or "True" Socialism

The socialist and communist literature of France, a literature that originated under the pressure of a bourgeoisie in power, and that was the expression of the struggle against this power, was introduced into Germany at a time when the bourgeoisie in that country had just begun its contest with feudal absolutism.

German philosophers, would-be philosophers and men of letters eagerly seized on this literature, only forgetting that when these writings immigrated from France into Germany, French social conditions had not immigrated along with them. In contact with

German social conditions this French literature lost all its immediate practical significance and assumed a purely literary aspect. Thus, to the German philosophers of the eighteenth century, the demands of the first French Revolution were nothing more than the demands of "Practical Reason" in general, and the utterance of the will of the revolutionary French bourgeoisie signified in their eyes the laws of pure will, of will as it was bound to be, of true human will generally.

The work of the German *literati* consisted solely in bringing the new French ideas into harmony with their ancient philosophical conscience, or rather, in annexing the French ideas without deserting their own philosophic point of view.

This annexation took place in the same way in which a foreign language is appropriated, namely, by translation.

It is well known how the monks wrote silly lives of Catholic saints *over* the manuscripts on which the classical works of ancient heathendom had been written. The German *literati* reversed this process with the profane French literature. They wrote their philosophical nonsense beneath the French original. For instance, beneath the French criticism of the economic functions of money, they wrote "alienation of humanity," and beneath the French criticism of the bourgeois state they wrote "dethronement of the category of the general," and so forth.

The introduction of these philosophical phrases at the back of the French historical criticisms they dubbed "Philosophy of Action," "True Socialism," "German Science of Socialism," "Philosophical Foundation of Socialism," and so on.

The French socialist and communist literature was thus completely emasculated. And, since it ceased in the hands of the German to express the struggle of one class with the other, he felt conscious of having overcome "French one-sidedness" and of representing, not true requirements, but the requirements of truth; not the interests of the proletariat, but the interests of human nature, of man in general, who belongs to no class, has no reality, who exists only in the misty realm of philosophical phantasy.

This German socialism, which took its schoolboy task so seriously and solemnly, and extolled its poor stock-in-trade in such mountebank fashion, meanwhile gradually lost its pedantic innocence.

The fight of the German and especially of the Prussian bourgeoisie against feudal aristocracy and absolute monarchy, in other words, the liberal movement, became more earnest.

By this, the long-wished-for opportunity was offered to "True" Socialism of confronting the political movement with the socialistic demands, of hurling the traditional anathemas against liberalism, against representative government, against bourgeois competition, bourgeois freedom of the press, bourgeois legislation, bourgeois liberty and equality, and of preaching to the masses that they had nothing to gain, and everything to lose, by this bourgeois movement. German socialism forgot, in the nick of time, that the French criticism, whose silly echo it was, presupposed the existence of modern bourgeois society, with its corresponding economic conditions of existence, and the political constitution adapted thereto, the very things whose attainment was the object of the pending struggle in Germany.

To the absolute governments, with their following of parsons, professors, country squires and officials, it served as a welcome scarecrow against the threatening bourgeoisie.

It was a sweet finish after the bitter pills of floggings and bullets, with which these same governments, just at that time, dosed the German working-class risings.

While this "True" Socialism thus served the governments as a weapon for fighting the German bourgeoisie, it, at the same time, directly represented a reactionary interest, the interest of the German philistines. In Germany the petty-bourgeois class, a relic of the sixteenth century, and since then constantly cropping up again under the various forms, is the real social basis of the existing state of things.

To preserve this class is to preserve the existing state of things in Germany. The industrial and political supremacy of the bourgeoisie threatens it with certain destruction—on the one hand, from the concentration of capital; on the other, from the rise of a revolutionary proletariat. "True" Socialism appeared to kill these two birds with one stone. It spread like an epidemic.

The robe of speculative cobwebs, embroidered with flowers of rhetoric, steeped in the dew of sickly sentiment, this transcendental robe in which the German Socialists wrapped their sorry "eternal truths," all skin and bone, served to wonderfully increase the sale of their goods amongst such a public. And on its part German socialism recognised, more and more, its own calling as the bombastic representative of the petty-bourgeois philistine.

It proclaimed the German nation to be the model

nation, and the German petty philistine to be the typical man. To every villainous meanness of this model man it gave a hidden, higher, socialistic interpretation, the exact contrary of its real character. It went to the extreme length of directly opposing the "brutally destructive" tendency of communism, and of proclaiming its supreme and impartial contempt of all class struggles. With very few exceptions all the so-called socialist and communist publications that now (1847) circulate in Germany belong to the domain of this foul and enervating literature.[1]

## 2. CONSERVATIVE OR BOURGEOIS SOCIALISM

A part of the bourgeoisie is desirous of redressing social grievances in order to secure the continued existence of bourgeois society.

To this section belong economists, philanthropists, humanitarians, improvers of the condition of the working class, organisers of charity, members of societies for the prevention of cruelty to animals, temperance fanatics, hole-and-corner reformers of every imaginable kind. This form of socialism has, moreover, been worked out into complete systems.

We may cite Proudhon's *Philosophie de la Misère* [*Philosophy of Poverty*] as an example of this form.

The socialistic bourgeois want all the advantages of modern social conditions without the struggles

[1] The revolutionary storm of 1848 swept away this whole shabby tendency and cured its protagonists of the desire to dabble in socialism. The chief representative and classical type of this tendency is Mr. Karl Grün. [*Note by F. Engels to the German edition of 1888.*]

and dangers necessarily resulting therefrom. They desire the existing state of society minus its revolutionary and disintegrating elements. They wish for a bourgeoisie without a proletariat. The bourgeoisie naturally conceives the world in which it is supreme to be the best; and bourgeois socialism develops this comfortable conception into various more or less complete systems. In requiring the proletariat to carry out such a system, and thereby to march straightway into the social New Jerusalem, it but requires in reality that the proletariat should remain within the bounds of existing society, but should cast away all its hateful ideas concerning the bourgeoisie.

A second and more practical, but less systematic, form of this socialism sought to depreciate every revolutionary movement in the eyes of the working class by showing that no mere political reform, but only a change in the material conditions of existence, in economical relations, could be of any advantage to them. By changes in the material conditions of existence, this form of socialism, however, by no means understands abolition of the bourgeois relations of production, an abolition that can be affected only by a revolution, but administrative reforms, based on the continued existence of these relations; reforms, therefore, that in no respect affect the relations between capital and labour, but, at the best, lessen the cost, and simplify the administrative work of bourgeois government.

Bourgeois socialism attains adequate expression when, and only when, it becomes a mere figure of speech.

Free trade: for the benefit of the working class.

Protective duties: for the benefit of the working class. Prison reform: for the benefit of the working class. This is the last word and the only seriously meant word of bourgeois socialism.

It is summed up in the phrase: the bourgeois is a bourgeois—for the benefit of the working class.

### 3. CRITICAL-UTOPIAN SOCIALISM AND COMMUNISM

We do not here refer to that literature which, in every great modern revolution, has always given voice to the demands of the proletariat, such as the writings of Babeuf and others.

The first direct attempts of the proletariat to attain its own ends, made in times of universal excitement, when feudal society was being overthrown; these attempts necessarily failed, owing to the then undeveloped state of the proletariat, as well as to the absence of the economic conditions for its emancipation, conditions that had yet to be produced, and could be produced by the impending bourgeois epoch alone. The revolutionary literature that accompanied these first movements of the proletariat had necessarily a reactionary character. It inculcated universal asceticism and social levelling in its crudest form.

The socialist and communist systems, properly so called, those of Saint-Simon, Fourier, Owen, and others, spring into existence in the early undeveloped period, described above, of the struggle between proletariat and bourgeoisie (see Section 1. Bourgeois and Proletarians).

The founders of these systems see, indeed, the

class antagonisms, as well as the action of the decomposing elements in the prevailing form of society. But the proletariat, as yet in its infancy, offers to them the spectacle of a class without any historical initiative or any independent political movement.

Since the development of class antagonism keeps even pace with the development of industry, the economic situation, as they find it, does not as yet offer to them the material conditions for the emancipation of the proletariat. They therefore search after a new social science, after new social laws, that are to create these conditions.

Historical action is to yield to their personal inventive action; historically created conditions of emancipation to fantastic ones; and the gradual, spontaneous class organisation of the proletariat to an organisation of society especially contrived by these inventors. Future history resolves itself, in their eyes, into the propaganda and the practical carrying out of their social plans.

In the formation of their plans they are conscious of caring chiefly for the interests of the working class, as being the most suffering class. Only from the point of view of being the most suffering class does the proletariat exist for them.

The undeveloped state of the class struggle, as well as their own surroundings, causes Socialists of this kind to consider themselves far superior to all class antagonisms. They want to improve the condition of every member of society, even that of the most favoured. Hence, they habitually appeal to society at large, without distinction of class; nay, by preference, to the ruling class. For how can people, when once they understand their system, fail to see in it the best possible plan of the best possible state of society?

Hence, they reject all political, and especially all revolutionary action; they wish to attain their ends by peaceful means, and endeavour, by small experiments, necessarily doomed to failure, and by the force of example, to pave the way for the new social gospel.

Such fantastic pictures of future society, painted at a time when the proletariat is still in a very undeveloped state and has but a fantastic conception of its own position, correspond with the first instinctive yearnings of that class for a general reconstruction of society.

But these socialist and communist publications contain also a critical element. They attack every principle of existing society. Hence they are full of the most valuable materials for the enlightenment of the working class. The practical measures proposed in them—such as the abolition of the distinction between town and country, of the family, of the carrying on of industries for the account of private individuals, and of the wage system, the proclamation of social harmony, the conversion of the function of the state into a mere superintendence of production—all these proposals point solely to the disappearance of class antagonisms which were, at that time, only just cropping up, and which, in these publications, are recognised in their earliest indistinct and undefined forms only. These proposals, therefore, are of a purely utopian character.

The significance of critical-utopian socialism and communism bears an inverse relation to historical development. In proportion as the modern class struggle develops and takes definite shape, this fantastic standing apart from the contest, these fantastic attacks on it, lose all practical value and all theoretical justification. Therefore, although the originators of these systems were, in many respects, revolutionary, their disciples have, in every case, formed mere reactionary sects. They hold fast by the original views of their masters, in opposition to the progressive historical development of the proletariat. They, therefore, endeavour, and that consistently, to deaden the class struggle and to reconcile the class antagonisms. They still dream of experimental realisation of their social utopias, of founding isolated *phalanstères*, of establishing "Home Colonies," or setting up a "Little Icaria"[1]—pocket editions of the New Jerusalem—and to realise all these castles in the air they are compelled to appeal to the feelings and purses of the bourgeois. By degrees they sink into the category of the reactionary conservative socialists depicted above, differing from these only by more systematic pedantry, and by their fanatical and superstitious belief in the miraculous effects of their social science.

They, therefore, violently oppose all political action on the part of the working class; such action, according to them, can only result from blind unbelief in the new gospel.

The Owenites in England, and the Fourierists in

---

[1] "Home colonies" were what Owen called his communist model societies. [*Added by F. Engels to the German edition of* 1890.] *Phalanstères* were socialist colonies on the plan of Charles Fourier; Icaria was the name given by Caber to his utopia and, later on, to his American communist colony. [*Note by F. Engels to the English edition of* 1888.]

France, respectively, oppose the Chartists and the *Réformistes*.

# IV • POSITION OF THE COMMUNISTS IN RELATION TO THE VARIOUS EXISTING OPPOSITION PARTIES

Section II has made clear the relations of the Communists to the existing working-class parties, such as the Chartists in England and the Agrarian Reformers in America.

The Communists fight for the attainment of the immediate aims, for the enforcement of the momentary interests of the working class; but in the movement of the present they also represent and take care of the future of that movement. In France the Communists ally themselves with the Social-Democrats[1] against the conservative and radical bourgeoisie, reserving, however, the right to take up a critical position in regard to phrases and illusions traditionally handed down from the Great Revolution.

In Switzerland they support the Radicals, without losing sight of the fact that this party consists of an-

---

[1] The party then represented in Parliament by Ledru-Rollin, in literature by Louis Blanc (1811–82), in the daily press by the *Réforme*. The name of Social-Democracy signifies, with these its inventors, a section of the Democratic or Republican Party more or less tinged with socialism. [*Note by F. Engels to the English edition of* 1888.]

tagonistic elements, partly of Democratic Socialists, in the French sense, partly of radical bourgeois.

In Poland they support the party that insists on an agrarian revolution as the prime condition for national emancipation, that party which fomented the insurrection of Cracow in 1846.

In Germany they fight with the bourgeoisie whenever it acts in a revolutionary way, against the absolute monarchy, the feudal squirearchy, and the petty-bourgeoisie.

But they never cease, for a single instant, to instil into the working class the clearest possible recognition of the hostile antagonism between bourgeoisie and proletariat, in order that the German workers may straightway use, as so many weapons against the bourgeoisie, the social and political conditions that the bourgeoisie must necessarily introduce along with its supremacy, and in order that, after the fall of the reactionary classes in Germany, the fight against the bourgeoisie itself may immediately begin.

The Communists turn their attention chiefly to Germany, because that country is on the eve of a bourgeois revolution that is bound to be carried out under more advanced conditions of European civilisation and with a much more developed proletariat than that of England was in the seventeenth, and of France in the eighteenth century, and because the bourgeois revolution in Germany will be but the prelude to an immediately following proletarian revolution.

In short, the Communists everywhere support every revolutionary movement against the existing social and political order of things.

In all these movements they bring to the front, as the leading question in each, the property question, no matter what its degree of development at the time.

Finally, they labour everywhere for the union and agreement of the democratic parties of all countries.

The Communists disdain to conceal their views and aims. They openly declare that their ends can be attained only by the forcible overthrow of all existing social conditions. Let the ruling classes tremble at a communist revolution. The proletarians have nothing to lose but their chains. They have a world to win.

Working men of all countries, unite!

## PLUME and MERIDIAN Titles of Related Interest

☐ **REVOLUTIONARIES by E. J. Hobsbawm.** A brilliant investigation of the theory and practice of revolution in the twentieth century. It traces the course of revolutionary ideology and action throughout the world——from Russia to Vietnam, from Spain to Cuba——describing and assessing goals, methods, successes, and failures, whether of political action, guerrilla warfare, or the individual act of violence.
(#F425—$3.95)*

☐ **LIVING MY LIFE by Emma Goldman. Edited by Richard and Marie Drinnon.** The brilliant autobiography of America's most famous anarchist.
(#F573—$8.95)*

☐ **HUMAN RIGHTS READER Edited by Walter Laqueur and Barry Rubin.** "A valuable resource in the current world-wide debate over human rights."—*Newsday*
(#F511—$6.95)*

☐ **FABLES AND FAIRYTALES by Leo Tolstoy. New translation by Ann Dunnigan. Foreword by Raymond Rosenthal, translator, Editor.** Twenty-nine stories including *The Mouse Who Lived Under the Granary, Equal Inheritance, Birds in a Net* and *A Last Judge.*
(#Z5302—$3.95)*

☐ **A HISTORY OF RUSSIA by John Lawrence.** This modern classic is a concise, readable narrative that spans 2,000 years of Russian History.
(#F488—$4.95)*

*In Canada, please add $1.00 to the price of each book.

---

**Buy them at your local**

**bookstore or use coupon**

**on next page for ordering.**

# MENTOR Titles of Interest

## MENTOR Books on the Orient

# The MENTOR Philosophers

A distinguished series presenting in historical order the basic writings of the outstanding philosophers of the Western world—from the Middle Ages to the present time.

☐ **THE AGE OF BELIEF: The Medieval Philosophers edited by Anne Fremantle.** Basic writings of the most important philosopher from the 5th to the 15th century, including St. Augustine, Boethius, Abelard, St. Bernard, St. Thomas Aquinas, Duns Scotus, William of Ockam and others. (#MJ1837—$1.95)

☐ **THE AGE OF REASON: THE 17th Century Philosophers selected and edited by Stuart Hampshire.** Selections from the basic writings of Descartes, Leibnitz, Spinoza and other great philosophers of "the century of Genius," when science began to influence philosophical thought. With penetrating Introduction and interpretive Commentary. (#MJ1872—$1.95)

☐ **THE AGE OF ENLIGHTENMENT: The 18th Century Philosophers, selected and edited by Isaiah Berlin.** Basic writings of Berkeley, Locke, Voltaire, Reid, Hume and other brilliant philosophers of the rational and humanistic age which believed that science's achievements could be translated into philosophical terms.
(#ME2003—$2.50)

☐ **THE AGE OF ANALYSIS: 20th Century Philosophers edited by Morton White.** Basic writings of Peirce, Whitehead, James, Croce, Santayana, Dewey, Sartre, and others, covering such problems as logic, philosophical and linguistic analysis, existentialism, phenomenology, and time. (#ME1847—$1.75)

---